LIVING
in the Light of Day

How to avoid the 'Success Trap', strive to be at your best and live a more meaningful, flourishing, and prosperous life.

David Penglase
B.Bus (HRD), MBA, MProfEthics, MScAPP

National Library of Australia Cataloguing-in-Publication data: Penglase, David, author.

Title: LIVING in the Light of Day / David Penglase

ISBN:

Paperback: 978-1-922691-88-0
Hardback: 978-1-922691-87-3
Ebook: 978-1-922691-89-7

Busybird Publishing
2/118 Para Road
Montmorency, Victoria
Australia 3094
www.busybird.com.au

Subjects:

Self-help. Communication. Relationships. Trust. Ethics. Business. Leadership. Positive Psychology.

In memory of my mother who left our
earth way too young.

Her love and moral example of what
it means to be truly
LIVING in the Light of Day
have been my guiding light and will
remain with me forever.

Contents

Praise

for David Penglase's
LIVING in the Light of Day

"From the opening reflections to the expansive list of 25 qualities of a good life, we are treated to a patient and understanding guide on how to grow into a trustworthy driver of your own life – and a trustworthy companion in the better world we all need to build together. While news stories abound of crooks and swindlers dodging consequences and living large on their crimes, Living in the Light of Day reminds us that true wealth, success, and happiness are built on a foundation of trust."

Michael F. Steger, PhD
Speaker, Professor, and Director of the Center for Meaning and Purpose
Colorado State University

"An insightful, illuminating, and above all helpful book on a topic of real importance that is often overlooked and underappreciated in our modern world"

Dr. Tim Lomas
Senior lecturer in positive psychology
University of East London

"David Penglase takes an established principle, Justice Brandeis' famous 'Sunlight Test', and invests it with additional depth and renewed relevance. His conclusion that a good life is one in which we become the best version of ourselves invites deep reflection - on many levels - in the best tradition of philosophy."

Dr Simon Longstaff AO
Executive Director, The Ethics Centre

"David's latest work couldn't come at a better time, but when you consider the subject matter he canvasses in Living in the Light of Day, when has his advice and observations not been relevant. In all of our relationships starting in the family home, business and

across countries the foundation of how we exist, conduct ourselves and thrive as a society is based on trust. With it we grow, without it we never reach full potential. I commend David on his work and believe society will be richer with his latest book."

Peter Baines OAM
Founder, Hands Across the Water.

"David Penglase invites you to live a happy, flourishing, and prosperous life by being courageous, taking action, focussing on what you want for others, giving them a reason to trust you, and being accountable for your actions. Nearly a decade ago he shared the power of Intentionomics with the world. Living in the Light of Day, comes at a moment of profound disruption and change. Let it be your guide to be the best version of yourself."

Olivia Sarah-Le Lacheur
Chair, AFA Foundation

"I loved this book from the moment I started reading it. It is such an important piece of work in a time when it appears we are losing our sense of direction and our understanding of what is truth and what is fiction. I encourage you to engage deeply with this elegant and enlightening guide to a better and more purposeful life."

Dr Adam Fraser.
Director of the e-Lab (TM)
Author of 'The Third Space' and 'Strive'

"As a former United Nations peacekeeper and military commander, I know the importance of trust, particularly when it comes to leading teams on the battlefield, where your decisions directly impact on the lives of others. Trust needs to be earnt and is an integral part of our lives, communities, and our world. David delivers a resourceful and insightful book that will help you become a better person, leader, and ultimately, become the best version of yourself."

Major Matina Jewell (retd)

"David has so eloquently found a way to capture and share the depth of his life's work and learnings. It is written in the way he lives, on Purpose, with Trust and Integrity. This book is for anyone that is committed to being the best human being they can be."

Larry Fingleson,
Co-founder and Managing Director The Growth Project
& Founder & CEO of The Catalytic Impact Institute

"This powerful book is rich with wisdom, brimming with compelling stories, and inspiring in its open invitation to you - the reader - to transform into a higher, more enlightened version of yourself. David's clear, honest voice doesn't just entreat you to evolve, he shows you how. A patient and wise guide, David shows you how to intentionally choose to become a better version of you."

G. Shawn Hunter
President, Mindscaling
Author, Small Acts of Leadership: 12 Intentional Behaviors That Lead to Big Impact

"David's book is a powerful reframe with practical strategies for leading a happy, fruitful life. Whether doubtful of the road ahead or looking to take life to the next level, this book provides more than band aids for challenges but a real strategy for life."

Jon Yeo
Curator TEDxMelbourne
Executive Speaker Coach

"There are so many self-help books these days that you can pick what you want to change and there will be a book for it. This book, however, is enlightening in the way that it addresses what we all need to get back TRUST. Trust in ourselves, others, and our purpose and then to live life to the fullest in the light of day."

Nicolette Barnard
Head of HR Pacific, Siemens

"Your time is limited, don't waste it living someone else's life."

Steve Jobs

Chapter One

Avoiding the success trap

Spoiler Alert! Not everyone can make it to the top … there's just not enough room!

Imagine, just for a moment, that almost everything you've been told about being successful was basically flawed.

Do you seriously believe you can be anything you want to be?

Really? Anything?

Motivational gurus around the globe extract millions of dollars from people wanting (needing) to believe in self-help spin like 'The Law of Attraction' – which is often defined as 'If you want something enough, it will miraculously manifest itself into your life'.

Good luck with that.

The problem is many of these flawed ideas and strategies around success, often have elements of truth and possibility about them. For this reason, they sound good, seem to make sense, are often unchallenged and many have become almost part of our modern psyche.

Consider this though. Amidst this push for positive thinking and the promise of success, data from many developed countries indicate that about 1 in every 5 working adults have mental health disorders and substance abuse problems. This rate increases to more than 1 in 3 people over a lifetime who will develop a behavioural health disorder.[1]

Things aren't quite right

Something in the way we are gauging success in life is awry.

What if the pursuit of success could make you feel like a failure and do serious damage to your sense of life satisfaction?

That's the Success Trap!

This doesn't mean positive thinking or being an optimist are wrong. However, as you will discover in this book, it's just not always appropriate.

This is also not suggesting setting goals is a bad idea. In fact, it's a good idea, but sometimes we set goals for all the wrong reasons and even when the goal is achieved your sense of success and life satisfaction may be at risk.

What are you basing your assessment of success and life satisfaction on?

Success Traps in Personal Life

There is nothing wrong in wanting the best that money can buy, high-end luxury items, the latest in technology, or to 'have it all'. However, science tells us your sense of life satisfaction and success depend on what's driving your passion to have it all.

Be very aware that it is in the financial interest of advertisers and marketers (and not necessarily in your best interests) that you fall into the success trap of wanting to keep up with the Joneses (whoever the Joneses might be).

These marketers and advertisers use influencing strategies that entice you to believe the grass is greener on the other side of the fence; that you need to upgrade your car; you need to move to a bigger home; you need the latest shinier phone; you need the designer clothes; you need that latest high-tech kitchen gadget that chops, churns, grates, juices, blends, steams, bakes, and fries.

They're urging you to get out your credit cards, buy now, pay later, amass more 'stuff' to feel more successful. However, what you will discover in this book is a mass of evidence-based research overwhelmingly challenges that notion.

To be clear though, the success trap isn't just set around amassing more material things in your life.

Success Traps at Work

In the business world, the success trap is set and if you're caught, it is ready to make you feel like a failure.

If you buy into the advice of the motivation movement, all of us need to be ambitious … if you're not climbing the corporate ladder or striving to build your own multi-million dollar business, you'll never be a success.

That just doesn't make sense.

Not everyone wants to be a leader or own their own business. Does that mean they are destined never to be satisfied with their life or feel like they're successful?

What does make sense is the levels of life satisfaction, meaning, purpose, well-being, and success we can experience when we strive to be our best versions of ourselves.

None of us is perfect, and we each only have what we have.

This is not to say that being ambitious is wrong.

Again, what the research shows is, your sense of life satisfaction and success depend on what's driving your ambition.

This is also not saying you need to avoid success. What you need to avoid is being trapped into a false sense of what success is for you. More is not always better. The view is not always the best from the top.

That brings us to one of the goals of this book which is to help ensure you don't get caught in the 'success trap', and potentially feeling like a failure, or the very least, dissatisfied with your level of success.

What Happens When People Get Caught in The Success Trap?

Success traps come in many shapes and sizes … and once caught, all have the potential to negatively impact your overall sense of life satisfaction.

In workplace settings, success traps can cause people to turn a blind eye to unfair, unethical, immoral, or illegal practices.

Success traps at work can result in the pursuit of profit at any cost … regardless of the damage done to employees, customers, suppliers, the community, or environment.

Success traps can create work cultures that over time lead to exposure and failure.

In our personal lives, success traps can lead to lies, deceit and breaches of personal trust … all resulting in damaged and often irreparable relationships between partners, between parents and their children, between siblings or relatives, and between friends or teammates.

Make no mistake here though, the pursuit of success can indeed be admirable or worthwhile in your personal and work life. However, the success trap is set to catch anyone who lacks mindful awareness of the intentions behind their pursuit of success … and the success trap is even more dangerous when any action, in the pursuit of success is knowingly and intentionally driven by ego and without any care of the impact of decisions and actions on others.

What Is Success Anyway?

For a topic that is covered so broadly throughout our personal and business lives, a clear definition of success is problematic.

What does become clear is this: Context matters.

How you define or determine success will depend on the context – on what part of your life you might be referring to.

You might define success in your business life on your daily achievements. Many people report feeling more successful crossing off a task when completed on their daily 'to do' list.

You might feel successful on the achievement of short, medium, or long term goals (whether set by yourself, or with your manager)[2].

Success at work might be when you get a promotion – whether it's one you've been seeking, or one that is bestowed on you as a pleasant surprise.

Or it could be you feel successful when simply doing your job.

Many people report feeling more successful when their job involves making life better for someone else in some sort of way. It could be a customer, a colleague, a manager, a supplier, or anyone for that matter.[3]

Similarly, how you define or determine your success will depend on the context you're referring to in your personal life.

People report feeling more successful when they achieve a personal life goal.[4] Examples include reaching a savings or investment target; realising they have found their life-partner; birth of a child; being a member of a winning sports team; or travelling to see one of the famous wonders of the world.

When do you feel more successful in your business or personal life?

A more important question is, why do you feel successful in those situations?

Unless you become more aware of what's driving your pursuit for success, in whatever context of your personal or business life, you will be at risk of getting caught in a Success Trap.

The real and present danger is you might be caught in a Success Trap and completely unaware that you are.

An Alternative Lens for Success

As you read this book, you will be able to consider success and life satisfaction through an alternative lens.

The typical lens in which many people view success is by comparing ourselves to others. This can include comparing our achievements, what we have, where we live, our physical appearance and other such comparisons.

Few people, if any, win the social comparison game … there will always be someone who has more or done more than you. That's why social comparison is often referred to as a zero-sum game. It's a game that is almost impossible to win.

The more appropriate, practical, and achievable lens to view success is through striving to be the best version of yourself.

This is a book about building character, earning trust, and acting with integrity ... a reminder and blueprint for intentionally and authentically striving to be the best version of yourself, and for living a meaningful, flourishing, and prosperous life.

It is a book about living a 'good' life.

The Moral Responsibility of Striving to be Your Best

This is also a book about being accountable for your actions.

Recognising that none of us is perfect, this is *not* a book about striving for perfection ... no one wins at that game.

A word of warning here and reality check; make no mistake, for most of us, me included, intentionally and authentically striving to be the best version of yourself is not easy, but so very rewarding and important for all our futures.

Each of us has a moral responsibility to intentionally and authentically strive to be the best version of ourselves. If we don't, we do a disservice to ourselves, our families and loved ones, to our friends, our community and to the world.

Choosing to intentionally and authentically strive to be the best version of yourself will require of you to have the courage to accept your imperfections, mistakes, and flaws.

That is not an easy task for any of us.

Living intentionally and authentically striving to be at your best isn't for the feint-hearted, and yet throughout history, philosophers and thought leaders have agreed that it is our moral duty as humans to do so.

At the same time as accepting your imperfections, mistakes, and flaws, you'll also need to have the courage to think differently, choose differently and act differently.

As I am writing these words, my own self-talk is chattering away telling me I have no right to even dare write this book. My self-talk is warning me that I'm setting myself up for failure and exposing my own imperfections, mistakes, and flaws to the world.

And yet, as I personally apply one of the many evidence-based positive psychology strategies outlined in this book, I can mindfully acknowledge and accept my self-talk and the mixed emotions I'm feeling and choose to continue writing anyway.

It is mindful, appropriate actions that support us striving to be the best version of ourselves that matter.

I don't have to do battle with my self-talk, although I do remind myself that my years of academic study resulting in degrees in business and human resource development, an MBA, a Master degree in Professional Ethics and Master of Science degree in Applied Positive Psychology are the fuel that feeds my motivation to share with you what science can tell us about choosing to intentionally and authentically strive to be the best version of ourselves, and to live meaningful, flourishing and prosperous lives.

The Choices You Make

For most of my adult life I have been fascinated, both academically and experientially, by what causes people to think, feel and act the way they do.

People fascinate me because:

- **we are so similar and yet so different**

- **we can be in a similar situation and yet our experiences of that situation can differ**
- **we can have similar possessions or wealth and yet differ in our happiness**
- **we can have similar educational opportunities and yet differ in our wisdom**
- **we can have similar opportunities and yet differ in how we use them**
- **we can have similar choices and yet make very different decisions.**

Many lessons have and continue to be learned from the Covid-19 global pandemic.

The lockdowns, isolations, border closures, travel restrictions and separation from loved ones has given many people time and opportunity to think about what's really important in their lives.

It's given people time to reflect on their lives, who they are, what they stand for, and how satisfied they are with the life they are living.

In disastrous situations like the Global pandemic, it becomes even more obvious why the world needs all of us to intentionally and authentically strive to be the best version of ourselves ... our future depends on it.

Imagine a world where every person had the courage to take up their moral duty to intentionally and authentically strive to be the best version of themselves ... to act with integrity, to be trustworthy, to be a person of good character.

While that might be impossible, the more of us who choose to be that person, the better this world will be.

You see, that's it isn't it … it's the choices we make and the actions we take that determine and show who we are, what really matters to us and what we stand for.

This then has been an introduction to the goals of this book … to challenge you to discover or rediscover what really matters in your life, avoid getting caught in the success trap and to strive to be the best version of yourself.

What's next?

In the pages that follow you will have the opportunity to reflect on the choices and actions you can make to strive to be the best version of yourself and ultimately how to live a meaningful, flourishing, and prosperous life.

In **chapter two** we further the discussion on the Success Trap and explore some examples of how people respond when caught out not striving to be at their best. We also look at the damage to relationships and trust and how that damage is difficult to repair, and the impact that can have on the success and life satisfaction of those involved.

In **chapter three** I will introduce you to a fresh look at the power of your *intentions.*

You will discover that your intentions are far more than just a thought about what you intend to do, and how your intentions can unlock the door to higher levels of meaning, purpose and yes … success in your professional and personal lives.

In **chapter four** I will guide you through some practical and evidence-based activities that will help you gain further clarity on the importance of intentions, and how to live a more intentional, meaningful, flourishing, and prosperous life.

In **chapter five** we will explore the links between intention and the levels of trust you experience in your work and personal relationships. I will introduce you to the ***Intentional Steps to Trust***™ process that covers five steps to help you earn, build, and maintain trust-based relationships.

I am certainly not saying these five Intentional Steps to Trust are guaranteed to solve all your relationship problems or lead you to living a more meaningful, flourishing, and prosperous life.

However, what I am saying is that these steps are each backed by evidence-based scientific research that will certainly help you to take appropriate action to positively affect your life – and the lives of those you impact through your professional and personal relationships.

In **chapter six** I will introduce you to three lenses through which you can consider trust in a very practical way. You will learn about the confidence and control required for self-trust; the courage and collaboration required to trust others; and the combined character, competence, and consistency required to earn others' trust.

Chapter seven is focused on the confidence and control required for self-trust. We will explore why self-trust is the trust upon which the other two types of trust rest. You will discover that if we do not get self-trust right in our lives, everything else starts to topple.

Chapter eight looks at the courage and collaboration required to trust others. You will discover why placing your trust blindly in others is a flawed practice because it opens the door to blame, criticism, mistakes, and loss of accountability.

Chapter nine delves into the combined character, competence and consistency required for you to earn others' trust. We will explore what is meant when we refer to someone's character, and why the old adage 'Promise what you can deliver and deliver on your promises' is still a powerful guiding principle to apply in all our relationships.

Rather than looking at success through a lens of social comparison to others, *Living in the Light of Day* reframes the lens of success by striving to be your best version of you and living a 'good life' … a meaningful, flourishing, and prosperous life.

There is such an enormous amount of research on what contributes to your overall sense of life satisfaction and in **Chapter ten** I have distilled this into 25 contributing elements to living a 'good life'. For each of these contributing elements, I provide you with some context, a key point, an activity, and the evidence you will experience as you complete the activity. I'm confident this will be a chapter you will return to again and again as you gain clarity on which of these contributing elements you would like to personally work on and enhance in your life.

The **final chapter** is a personal message from me, exploring the importance of making our lives more meaningful, and our moral duty to strive to be the best version of ourselves.

That is a rundown on what you are about to read, so let's begin by taking a deeper look into what happens when people do get caught in the Success Trap and when they choose not to strive to be the best version of themselves.

Chapter One Summary

Approach success in your business and personal life through a lens of striving to be the best version of yourself. The Success Trap is chasing success in any area of your life for all the wrong reasons – social comparison and being pressured to 'keep up with the Joneses' can just cause you unnecessary stress, anxiety and overwhelm.

"It's discouraging to think how many people
are shocked by honesty and
how few by deceit."

Noël Coward

Chapter Two

Mistake or intentional deception

As you've just read, taking intentional action to avoid the success trap of social comparison and view success through the lens of striving to be at your best, is not for the feint hearted.

It's not easy and there's a big chance you will make mistakes along the way.

We all make mistakes, and most of us are willing to admit we make mistakes. I certainly know I have ... some with more serious consequences than others.

I think you would agree that to make a mistake is just part of our imperfection as humans.

However, what if a mistake is not really a mistake? What if it is an intentional choice that was based mostly on the hope of not being caught?

What if it was an intentional choice – a gamble that someone was or is willingly taking – knowing that if they get caught it will negatively impact themselves and others?

Is that a mistake or intentional deception?

There is a big difference between an unintentional mistake and an intentional deception, and the difference between the two says a lot about a person's character, integrity, and trustworthiness.

Throughout history and continuing to the present we see a steady stream of individuals representing themselves, a sport, a religion, a company, an educational institution, or a profession being 'caught out' intentionally doing the wrong thing and only offering an apology because they'd been caught out.

It might not be easy to accept, but each of us is capable of doing wrong, even when we are aware that it is wrong.

You might be thinking "Not me!", but history and a long list of evidence-based research challenges that thought.

This then is a call, a reminder, to help you live up to your "Not me!" defence.

Unintentional mistakes and intentional deceptions often negatively impact relationships… the relationship you have with yourself and your relationships with others.

Central to most relationships is trust … the trust you have in yourself, the trust you place in other people and the trust that others place in you … your trustworthiness.

Trust is more complex than most of us think and as my friend and author Vanessa Hall says, "Trust is fragile"[5]. The reality is also that while most of us understand how important trust is to our success in relationships and life, we don't always get it right.

When we talk of breaches of trust, we are talking about relationships that have been fractured or broken because of either an unintentional mistake or an intentional deception.

So, let's take a look at relationships for a moment.

Relationships matter

From way back as cave dwellers to the current day, we humans have learned that relationships matter.

As cave dwellers it was a matter of survival – strength in numbers to fend off and protect each other from being the next meal of the day for some prehistoric animal.

While today most of us are not living with the constant danger of a sabre-toothed tiger around the corner, our relationships and reliance on others is just as important.

We need to trust ourselves and each other for our very survival.

Of all the contributing elements to living a good life, one of the most significant is the relationships you have with yourself and with others.

Are there relationships in your professional and personal life that you would readily say are flourishing, and that you find great joy, meaning and satisfaction from? Are there relationships that are not going so well? How is your relationship with yourself?

Let me return to the earlier discussion on breaches of trust and consider the value of the apologies.

When a CEO, politician, clergy, schoolteacher, sports star, or celebrity is reported on traditional or social media getting caught out intentionally breaching trust, they often apologise – but only in hindsight after being caught out.

Apologising in hindsight

Apologising 'in hindsight' can be an honourable reflection of a person's good character, when they are demonstrating they have made a genuine and unintentional mistake and are truly sorry.

However, it is a different story altogether when *in the moment* a person knowingly breaches someone's trust, they know what they are about to do is wrong, and yet they do it in the hope that they won't get caught.

And when they get caught, they apologise, but only because they've been caught.

This is totally different from a genuine and unintentional mistake and is usually seen for what it is ... a poor excuse and an insincere apology by someone who has just been caught out.

Let's consider some examples.

Drugs in sport

In 2013, after Lance Armstrong publicly admitted to using banned performance-enhancing drugs during his seven wins of the Tour de France, in an interview with Oprah Winfrey, he said: "I view this situation as one big lie I repeated a lot of times".

He went on to say: "I made those decisions; they were my mistake and I'm here to say sorry".

Armstrong was stripped of his titles and medals and stepped down as Chair of the Livestrong Foundation.[6]

Extramarital affairs

In 2011, when news broke that movie star and former Governor of California Arnold Schwarzenegger had been having an affair with a long-time staff member, and was the father of her child, he reportedly said: "I understand and deserve the feelings of anger and disappointment among my friends and family. There are no excuses and I take full responsibility for the hurt I have caused. I have apologized to Maria, my children, and my family. I am truly sorry".

Schwarzenegger and his then wife of 25 years are now divorced.[7]

Banks behaving badly

In 2019, former CEO of the National Australia Bank Andrew Thorburn was criticised by Commissioner Kenneth Hayne of the Royal Commission into Misconduct in the Banking, Superannuation and Financial Services Industry, for portraying the charging of fees for no service as a "product of poor systems and carelessness" and "just professional negligence".

Thorburn stepped down as CEO, reportedly saying he was "deeply sorry".[8]

Misuse of Private Details

In 2018, Facebook CEO Mark Zuckerberg apologised at a US Congress hearing for failing to protect the personal data of millions of users in the Cambridge Analytica scandal.

As detailed in the Congress hearing transcript reported in The Washington Post, Zuckerberg made this apology:

"We didn't take a broad enough view of our responsibility, and that was a big mistake. And it was my mistake. And I'm sorry. I started Facebook, I run it, and I'm responsible for what happens here."

Defrauding Investors in Medical Breakthrough

In 2014, healthcare technology company Theranos and its CEO, Elizabeth Holmes, were on top of the world. The rise and rise of Theranos saw Holmes become the youngest self-made female billionaire at the time. However, only a few years later it all came crashing down.

Through a number of investigations, it was discovered that the technology used by Theranos to test blood for a range of illnesses and diseases had a number of shortcomings and was not as accurate as being claimed and the role Holmes had played in covering it all up was exposed.

In January 2022, a California jury found the 37 year old Holmes guilty on three counts of fraud and one count of conspiring to defraud private investors. At the time of writing, Holmes was to be sentenced later in the year.

Unlike Armstong, Schwarzenegger, Thorburn and Zuckerberg, Holmes has not apologised and while still claiming her innocence during the trial said, "I know that we made mistakes."[9]

The jury's verdict would suggest they weren't mistakes, but rather, intentional deception.

What if we lived in a world where intentional deception did not exist?

What if we lived in a world where people's choices and actions were based on what is moral, just, legal, fair, and transparent?

While I realise that is almost if not impossible, there is a way for you, me, and others to make better and more intentional choices and actions.

What impact might that have on our overall sense of life satisfaction and success in our professional and personal lives?

Living in the light of day

Dr Simon Longstaff from The Ethics Centre (formerly the St James Ethics Centre) in Sydney was a guest lecturer who first shared with me, and my Master of Professional Ethics cohort, an approach to ethical decision-making. It was based on the *Sunlight Test,* which was most famously articulated in the nineteen thirties by Justice Brandeis of the US Supreme Court.

Brandeis is attributed as writing "If the broad light of day could be let in upon men's actions, it would purify them as the sun disinfects."[10]

The Sunlight Test points out the importance of only doing those things that we would be proud of if held up in the light of day, rather than do what might be popular.

In an article written by Anthony Pagano PhD, titled 'Criteria for Ethical Decision Making in Managerial Situations', rather than using the term 'Sunlight Test', he referred to it as the 'Light of Day Test'.[11]

In that article, Pagano explained the Light of Day Test in this way: "Suppose that the decision or action that is contemplated became a featured story on the local news. Would you be proud, or would you fear public exposure?"

I personally prefer to use the term *Light of Day Test*, and having considered and researched this on various levels over many years. I would like to share my version of the Light of Day Test with you now:

With any decision you're about to make, or any action you're about to take, would you make that decision or take that action if it were held up in the light of day for all to see?

Among many great lessons over my many years of academic study, especially in the areas of professional ethics and positive psychology, the Light of Day Test was and continues to be one of the most important.

Better decision making ***in the moment***

I wonder if Armstrong, Schwarzengger, Thorburn, Zuckerberg, and Holmes had applied the Light of Day Test at the time of their indiscretions, could things have been different?

Maybe yes. Maybe no.

Either way, in each of these cases, choosing intentional deceit had serious consequences.

To be clear here ... avoiding being found out is ***not*** what the Light of Day Test is about. It is about knowing the difference between right and wrong and what a person of 'good' character would choose to do ... and choosing to do that.

In the cases of Zuckerberg, Thorburn and Holmes, it can be said that not every CEO knows everything that is going on in a large corporation. But someone (more likely many) knew, and it is certainly obvious that whoever did know did not apply the Light of Day Test.

Of course, these examples of companies, their CEO's, leaders, and employees behaving badly are not isolated incidents when it comes to big business.

In a July 2018 lecture titled 'Companies Behaving Badly', Australian Competition and Consumer Commission (ACCC) Chair Rod Sims listed a number of "well known and respected companies" who have admitted, or been found, to have breached competition and consumer laws".

Included in Sims' list of companies behaving badly were:

Ford admitting to engaging in unconscionable conduct in the way they treated customer complaints about their cars shuddering with Powershift transmission. Ford were ordered to pay $10 million in penalties.

Telstra's third-party billing service exposing mobile phone customers to unauthorised charges. Telstra was also ordered to pay $10 million in penalties.

Thermomix making false or misleading representations to some customers over a safety issue by remaining silent when knowing about the fault. Thermomix was ordered to pay over $4.5 million in penalties.

Flight Centre attempting to induce three international airlines to enter into price-fixing agreements. Flight Centre was ordered to pay $12.5 million in damages.

It is worth also noting that these examples of companies being caught out behaving badly were from just one month, April 2018.

The list, as Sims put it, was unfortunately "just the tip of the iceberg".

He went on in his speech to identify big name companies such as:

Heinz for misleading consumers regarding a product they claimed was good for children, when two-thirds of the ingredients was sugar.

Reckitt Benckiser for misleading consumers (and charging higher prices) by marketing four different versions of their Nurofen product to treat different types of pain, when each product contained the same active ingredient.

Sims also 'called out' **Meriton, Optus, Pental, Kimberly-Clark, Coles, Bet365, and Acquire Learning and Careers** for breaches of trust, misleading claims, or unconscionable conduct.

I know you will recognise many of these large organisations, and you would be right to be shaking your head in disbelief.

If you were to read any of the annual reports of these companies you would find, somewhere near their Vision and Values Statements, a statement regarding how much they value their customers.

Indeed, that was Sims' observation as well, when he said: "These same companies regularly proclaim they put their customers first".[12]

For companies behaving badly, being caught out – and apologising in hindsight – is a costly matter, and not just from a financial perspective.

Yes … hindsight apologies are much easier, but a more mindful decision ***in the moment*** is surely better.

Now there are of course those who will want to jump in and say that Schwarzenegger has gone on to continue a successful career, and the consequences of his actions haven't really impacted him that negatively.

It could even be argued that he is not an exception – that others who have been caught out performing intentional acts of deceit also continue or transform their lives or careers for the better.

Defrauding investors

You could argue this is the case with the real 'Wolf of Wall Street', Jordan Belfort.

Journalist Katherine Rushton reported on Belfort's fall from grace in this way: "As the founder of Stratton Oakmont, a brokerage firm, he defrauded investors of more than $US100 million and then turned in his co-conspirators to cut his own jail term. His firm was closed in 1998 and he served 22 months in prison".

Belfort shared in an interview with Rushton (and other interviews to whoever would give him airplay or screen time) his way of morally disengaging from what he did by saying, "I don't want to come off like what I did was not wrong. It was wrong. But I wasn't dealing with poor people, I was dealing with very rich people. No one lost their life savings".[13]

Yeah … right!

Belfort, claiming to have turned his life around, became a motivational speaker on the international conference speaking circuit, spruiking the same negotiation, influencing, and sales techniques he used to allegedly defraud those 'rich people'.

Schwarzenegger and Belfort may be examples of people who have intentionally deceived and still done ok – maybe even turned their lives around.

Indeed, in that same interview, Rushton quoted Belfort as saying: "Long term, scumbags don't make money. They get in trouble, and they do drugs, and they feel guilty about it. I believe in karma. If I could do it over, I would definitely take a completely different path".

Humans make mistakes and humans can redeem themselves from those mistakes – whether from intentionally deceiving or from unintentional mistakes.

Just as an aside, I'm wondering how many organisation CEOs who decided to send their salespeople along to a Jordan Belfort seminar on how to influence customers, would transparently and proudly write out to all of their customers informing them that their company's salespeople were being trained by the Wolf of Wall Street on how to sell, persuade, influence, and negotiate.

My point is ... sure, there will be examples of people making mistakes and making amends, and that is all very positive and ok. However, it is so often just done in hindsight. It is done reactively ... and much of the damage that was done will almost always linger and may never be fully remedied.

Surely the focus ought not only be on how we go about rectifying our wrongs (intentional or unintentional) ... surely we need to be more proactive and not just focus on how to rebuild trust when we stuff up.

So, let's be a bit more proactive here.

While everyone makes mistakes – and often unintentional mistakes that can result in a breach of trust – rather than learning how to reactively deal with cleaning up the mess of breaches of trust, let's be more intentional ***in the moment*** and apply the Light of Day Test.

You and the Light of Day Test

By applying the Light of Day Test more often in your life, you will become more skilled, confident, and comfortable with your everyday choices and actions, because you will have mindfully considered their impact, not only on yourself, but also on others.

This is the difference between falling into the Success Trap and pursuing success for all the wrong reasons (and the carnage it can leave in its wake) and striving to be the best version of you and enhance your sense of life satisfaction.

Throughout this book you will have the opportunity to explore how living in the light of day will positively impact your professional and personal life.

You will discover how it can, among many positive impacts, help you:

- **gain more clarity in an increasingly disruptive world**
- **develop more positive, nurturing, collaborative, and trust-based relationships**
- **better manage business and personal goal achievement**
- **bring more meaning and purpose into your life**

- **build your sense of confidence and pride in who you are**

- **help you live an even more flourishing and prosperous professional and personal life.**

I know that is a big claim, but the research I will be sharing with you validates the many possibilities and opportunities for you.

Beyond the ethical application of the Light of Day Test, think about the powerful imagery of these five words… in the light of day.

In the light of day, we experience the warmth from the sun. In the light of day is where growth occurs in nature.

And, in the light of day things become clearer for all to see.

It's in this metaphoric clarity of Living in the Light of Day, that things become clearer for you and others to see. Decisions seem less complex. Problems seem more solvable. Opportunities become more apparent.

And it's in this metaphoric clarity of Living in the Light of Day that you get to strive toward being your authentic and best self … the real you.

This is your opportunity to genuinely, intentionally, and authentically strive to be the best version of you.

In a LinkedIn article posted by the former Chair and CEO of PepsiCo, Indra Nooyi, she shares this wisdom and advice: "I encourage you: be mindful of your choices on the road ahead".[14]

As Nooyi points out, it's by making mindful choices, decisions and taking intentional action in the light of day – in the moments that matter most in your everyday life – that you demonstrate who you are and what you represent, and what you bring to the people you influence in your world.

Wisdom like that shared by Nooyi is everywhere, and wisdom wants you to find it.

Sometimes wisdom becomes apparent during a movie, or watching TV, or on social media, or just walking in a park. For me, it often leaps off pages in books or research articles.

Just one example where wisdom decided to show itself, was while I was studying philosophy.

I had just become a father for the second time. Our first son, Matthew, was three years old and the day after his third birthday our second son, Anthony, was born.

A few weeks after Anthony was born, I was in the university library reading the philosophical teaching of Aristotle, when these words he had written all those years ago leaped off the page at me:

"Our actions and our behaviours are our morals shown in conduct".

This is what Living in the Light of Day is all about. Everything we say, everything we do is sending loud and clear messages to the world about who we are and what we represent.

I realised as a father that my sons would grow up seeing my morals, my values, my principles, my ethics, my character on display, through my intentions, my words, my promises, my actions, and my behaviour.

You will not be too surprised to know, despite my best intentions, that I readily admit I haven't always lived up to be the best version of myself … as I've said, none of us is perfect.

As new parents at the time, my wife Liz and I set some family guidelines by which we and our children would relate with each other. One such guideline was "We as family members will never yell at each other".

By the time Anthony had turned three we had changed the guideline to "We as family members will *try* to not yell at each other".

Please understand, my point in sharing this light-hearted reality in our lives is to say that this book is not intended to be a moralistic sledgehammer.

Rather, my intention is to remind and challenge you to be grateful for the relationships you have in your life, and to provide you with some evidence-based research, tips, and examples on how to make good (ethical) decisions, build your character and develop more positive and nurturing relationships in your personal and professional lives.

Over many years now, both academically and experientially, I've been researching and discovering links in philosophy, positive psychology, and behavioural science that can help guide us to strive toward being the best version of ourselves as often as possible.

Here is what I know …

People will get your truth! Over time, your intentions, promises, actions and results will either promote you as someone they can trust, or expose you as being untrustworthy.

It is in the Light of Day that people determine the extent to which they will trust you and the type of relationship they want to have with you.

By now you will have already noticed a number of interconnected themes including ethics, integrity, intention, relationships, and trust, which are just some of the contributing elements to living a meaningful, flourishing, and prosperous life.

As you continue reading, you will discover how these interconnected themes are impacting all of our lives.

However, at this stage there is one contributing element that is not only central to almost everything else we will explore together in this book, but also central to almost all we do in our lives… trust.

We first need to agree that trust is something we most certainly ought to be bothered about.

Trust matters because it is central to almost every relationship we have in our professional and personal lives.

For most of my adult life I have been fascinated by, and researching both academically and experientially, how our relationships impact our sense of wellbeing and overall life satisfaction.

Again, put simply, trust matters because relationships matter!

Aside from my research, at the time of writing, I have been personally blessed with being happily and gratefully married to my wife and best friend, Liz, for 38 years.

We have also been working together in our own corporate education and conference-speaking business for over 28 years.

So, over many years now, I have learned a thing or two experientially about relationships.

Just as importantly, though, for most of my adult life I have also been academically researching and studying the impact of the relationships we have with ourselves and with others.

I think it's important I acknowledge that for Liz and me, working together, living together, raising two sons who are now adults, has mostly been a joy, but that's not to say it has always been easy, or that we've got it all worked out.

But you already know that don't you. Relationships are not always easy!

Maybe not easy, but necessary ... our very existence and life satisfaction depend on them.

An ever-growing body of evidence-based research highlights that having positive, supportive, and nurturing relationships is associated with a host of important elements that contribute to our capacity to flourish in our personal and professional lives.

Good relationships are good for us physically.

Researching the impact of positive relationships on health and mortality, in just one study reviewing 81 other studies on relationships, Professor Bert Uchino from the University of Utah, and his colleagues,[15] found consistent associations with good relationships and positive increased functioning of our heart (cardiovascular), glandular (endocrine), and immune systems.

Good relationships are good for us psychologically.

Extensive research conducted by two of the recognised founders of the field of positive psychology, Ed Diener and Martin Seligman, shows that positive relationships also have strong associations with our sense of happiness and life satisfaction.[16]

Good relationships are good for us motivationally.

One of the most exciting applied theories of motivation to emerge over the past few decades is the result of research by Edward Deci and Richard Ryan.[17]

What they and hundreds of other researchers across the globe have discovered is that having positive and nurturing relationships, professionally and personally, is one of three core needs we have to flourish in life. The other two elements are a sense of competency and a sense of autonomy.

We will investigate Deci's and Ryan's research a little more in chapter seven on self-trust.

What I have presented to you so far is just the tip of the vast evidence-based research that shows the physical, psychological, and motivational benefits we can derive from having positive, supportive, and nurturing relationships.

This ought to be reason enough for us to bother about trust, but as they say in the television sales ads, "Wait, there is more".

Good relationships boost our sense of meaning and purpose.

The amazing work of Viktor Frankl,[18] who survived the horrors of Nazi war camps during World War II, is one of the most referenced research studies on how our relationships impact our sense of meaning and purpose, and how our very existence relies on and can be sustained by our positive relationships.

Frankl wrote in his internationally acclaimed book, *Man's Search for Meaning:*

"The salvation of man is through love and in love. I understood how a man who has nothing left in this world may still know bliss, be it only for a brief moment, in the contemplation of his beloved".

That is one of the most beautiful and inspiring quotes I know.

Albeit for just a 'brief moment' while in a concentration camp, as Frankl tuned his mind out from the horrific situation he found himself in, he could think of his beloved wife, and in that moment could 'still know bliss'.

Most of us will not face the adversity that Frankl did.

However, Frankl reminds us just how important it is for us to hold onto, cherish and be grateful for the positive relationships we have in our lives.

Through the global Covid-19 pandemic many countries' citizens were required to work from home. Many experienced extended periods of isolation and lockdowns. Through those experiences, many had the opportunity to pause, consider or rediscover the true value and meaning we experience through our personal relationships.

Relationships and trust are so much more than just feelings.

I could continue in this chapter with what might seem to you an over-justification of why we need to bother about relationships and why we need to bother about trust.

I'm fairly certain you don't need me to convince you that relationships matter in your life.

However, keeping them at the forefront of your intentions, promises and actions will result in you earning, building, and maintaining more trust-based relationships, and living an even more meaningful, flourishing, and prosperous professional and personal life.

Keeping your relationships and the importance of trust in your life at top of mind ought not be that difficult. However, the global communications firm Edelman, report that we live in a world where distrust has become the norm.[19]

Are we losing the capacity to trust?

Whether it is in mainstream or social media, we seem to be bombarded with the reporting of regular breaches of our trust, and this is having a significant and negative impact on our capacity to trust.

In Rachel Botsman's book, *Who Can You Trust? How technology brought us together and why it might drive us apart,* she suggests, "We are at the start of the third, biggest revolution in the history of humankind".[20]

Revolutions happen when people are disrupted to the point where they take action to fix what they see as the problem.

The loss of trust in our major institutions on a global level has reached a point where, as Botsman warns, "Fear, suspicion and disenchantment are deadly viruses that spread fast".

And so, we are seeing this fear and virus of distrust in major institutions and organisations spreading.

Organisations do not behave... people do

However, I want to make this point again ... Organisations do not 'behave' – people do.

There is a danger that we almost disassociate unethical behaviour occurring within local and global institutions of government, media, charities, businesses, or religious institutions from the reality that it's people who are acting unethically.

Consider these mainstream newspaper headlines:[21]

Ethics in banking? That's a negative.

Volkswagen scandal!

Facebook facing data breach investigation by regulator after hack.

While I understand the practicality of using institutional terms such as banking, Volkswagen, and Facebook, what I'm most concerned about is how using an organisational or institutional name detracts from the reality that people, either individually or collectively, act … organisations don't.

In the Final Report of the Royal Commission into Misconduct in the Banking, Superannuation and Financial Services Industry in Australia, Commissioner Kenneth Hayne wrote:[22]

"There can be no doubt that the primary responsibility for misconduct in the financial services industry lies with the entities concerned and those who managed and controlled those entities: their boards and senior management".

Hayne then highlights that while it is true that individually and collectively the board members and senior management hold that primary responsibility, "it is those who engage in misconduct who are responsible for what they did and for the consequences that followed".

Individual responsibility

Commissioner Hayne is highlighting the importance of individual responsibility.

Rather than delve more deeply into the institutional breaches of trust that have put trust at risk on a global scale, this book is aimed squarely at you, me, and our individual and collective capacity to live more *in the Light of Day* – to make ethical decisions, to build our character, and to develop more positive relationships in our professional and personal lives.

So, together now, let's explore one strategy that all other strategies will depend on to help you strive to be your best version of you and help you live a meaningful, flourishing, and prosperous life.

Chapter Two Summary

None of us is perfect. We all make mistakes but apologizing only in hindsight of being caught out for an intentional deception rarely makes things better. Damaged trust is hard to repair. To make better choices that represent you at your best use the Light of Day test by asking "With this decision I'm about to make, or this action I'm about to take, would I make the decision or take the action, if they were held up in the Light of Day for all to see?"

"Eventually, if there isn't deep integrity and fundamental character strength, the challenges of life will cause true motives to surface and human relationship failure will replace short-term success."

Stephen R. Covey

Chapter Three

The science of intention

The quote on the left from Stephen R. Covey is from the first chapter of his best-selling book, *The 7 Habits of Highly Effective People*,[23] and it is the perfect introduction for this chapter on intention.

Covey is warning us that our true motives 'eventually' will surface, and if they are not based on 'deep integrity and fundamental character strength', trust is put at risk and relationships will fail.

My aim is that by the end of this chapter you will understand the importance and impact of your intentions on almost every measure of success in your professional and personal life.

Intention matters because relationships matter.

You know when you first meet someone and you get that feeling, almost immediately, that you know you're going to get along with them just fine – you feel like they're someone you can trust … you're not quite sure why, but you feel it in your gut.

And then, on other occasions, you meet someone and this time you get a different feeling – a feeling that there's just something about this person you don't trust … again, you're not quite sure what it is, but there's just something about them.

Well, after my many years of academic research and study, I am convinced that a lot of that feeling we get about a person's trustworthiness comes down to what the scientific community refer to as *unconscious intelligence*,[24] or what most of us just call *intuition.*

Historically, from cave dwellers to modern time, we have been gathering data from our experiences, and through generation after generation our brains have been storing and passing on this data that forms our intuition or unconscious intelligence.

So, the 'feeling' you get when you first meet someone – whether you feel you can trust them or not – that feeling comes from your unconscious intelligence – yes … male and female intuition.

Just on that point, what do you think about the commonly held view that women use their intuition more often and with better results than men?

I can say from personal experience – and despite my extensive research into these areas – I have no doubt that Liz's intuition and unconscious intelligence about people is much stronger (and more often right) than my own.

And it seems science backs up that women use their intuition more often and with better results than men.

Researchers Tim Kaiser, Marco Del Giudice and Tom Booth accessed data from over 31,000 personality profiles worldwide to answer the fundamentally age-old question of whether men and women think, feel, and act differently.[25]

From a list of 15 personality traits (warmth, emotional stability, assertiveness, gregariousness, dutifulness, friendliness, sensitivity, distrust, imagination, reserve, anxiety, complexity, introversion, orderliness, emotionality), one of their main findings was on the 'sensitivity' scale.

That scale includes sensitive, aesthetic, sentimental, intuitive, and tender-minded, versus utilitarian, objective, unsentimental, and tough minded.

Their findings concluded that women scored higher than men on the sensitivity scale (which includes 'intuition') and therefore support the commonly held view that women are more intuitive than men.

What the research is not saying is that only women have 'intuition' or 'unconscious intelligence' ... men most certainly do as well. The research is also not confirming how often using intuition alone versus objectivity alone (by a male or female), reaps better results.

What is important here is acknowledging that there is such a thing as intuition; we all have it to a greater or lesser extent; we all use it to a greater or lesser extent; and most of us have experienced it when we meet other people for the first time – we get a feeling as to whether we trust them or not.[26]

What's going on here is that we are using our unconscious intelligence to make a quick judgment, based on a range of clues our brains have gathered over centuries, but also drawing on clues in that current moment when we first meet the person.

One of the key judgments our unconscious intelligence is trying to assess about this person is their intention – the real motive behind their words and actions.

And this intuition about people's intentions happens very quickly.

How quickly? That is what researchers Nalini Ambadi and Robert Rosenthal set out to discover. What they found was that we can make appraisals about the intentions of others, on average, in less than 30 seconds.[27]

Supporting these findings, researcher Alysha Baker and her colleagues wanted to know how quickly we make decisions about a person's trustworthiness just based on our perceptions of how they look.

What they found was that our evaluations of trustworthiness, based on a stranger's face, can be as quick as 38 milliseconds. Wow, that is quick, isn't it. The problem is, what they also found was that while we might be very quick at making up our mind about a person's intentions and trustworthiness, if we're only doing it based on first appearances we typically only get it right about half the time.[28]

So, while we naturally and instinctively use our unconscious intelligence or intuition to determine people's trustworthiness and their intentions, we need to realise that, while trusting our own 'gut feeling', at times we might be judging others too quickly.

For that reason, if we are so quick to judge a person's intentions (upon which we then judge their trustworthiness), we need to have a clear understanding of what it is we are in fact judging.

This chapter is a deep dive into what I refer to as the New Science of Intention and understanding your own and others' intentions is key to you living in the light of day and flourishing in life.

As I write this chapter, and having rewritten, edited, and rewritten it several times, I felt I needed to start with somewhat of a challenge to you.

One of my 'mentors-from-a-distance' (meaning I never personally met them, but they have positively influenced my life through their teaching) is the late Jim Rohn.[29] Sadly, Jim died in 2009, but his legacy as a philosopher, business educator, and motivational speaker continues through his books and recorded programs.

Among many of my favourite quotes from Jim is this:

"Don't just read the easy stuff. You may be entertained by it, but you will never grow from it".

I am sharing that quote with you because this chapter digs quite deeply, both scientifically and philosophically, into the true meaning of intention.

I could have skimmed over some of the detail you'll be presented with, but I thought you deserved the opportunity to dive deep into the content, and hope you'll be enriched by doing so.

So remember Jim's quote and know that my intention is to give you a deeper understanding of how and why your intentions are so important to you living in the light of day, and experiencing a meaningful, flourishing, and prosperous life.

Ok ... enough of the 'disclaimer' and onto the good stuff.

In a song titled '4 Minutes', sung by Madonna and featuring Justin Timberlake and Timbaland, one of the lines Madonna sings is the often-quoted proverb, 'The road to hell is paved with good intentions'.

What might this mean?

One interpretation is that you might have good intentions, but unless they are acted upon, positive outcomes may not be achieved.

For example, you might intend to lose weight, but despite your 'good' intention, you keep eating fatty and sugary foods and you end up putting on more and more weight.

This interpretation may point to the reason why much of the western world is facing an obesity epidemic. Obesity is not occurring from a lack of good intention, but rather from a lack of intentional action.[30]

Another interpretation of 'The road to hell is paved with good intentions' is that bad outcomes can occur despite one's best or good intention.

For example, in the Australian state of Queensland, early in the twentieth century, sugar-cane farmers were concerned about the damage to their crops from beetles. With all good intention, the Queensland Department of Agriculture introduced cane toads as a 'natural' way to rid the crops of the beetles.

The outcome has been a devastating cane toad 'plague' that the authorities never intended as an outcome and are still trying to find a solution to this day.[31]

And yet another interpretation of 'The road to hell is paved with good intentions' is that one person's good intentions may be another's worst nightmare.

Arguably Hitler could have strongly believed he had a 'good' intention to create a 'better' Germany. The negative and devastating impact on so many lives certainly challenge the notion of any 'good intention'.

There may be other ways to interpret this proverb, but what it does signify is the importance of understanding what we really mean when we speak about intentions and certainly what is meant by 'good' intentions.

To clear up the 'good' in good intentions, I subscribe to the overarching human value of 'First do no harm'.

In other words, a good intention is one that has the aim of doing no harm to anyone and, I would add, to positively create value and make life better in some way for the person toward whom the intention is aimed.

In a paper titled 'Trust, Legitimacy & The Ethical Foundations of the Market Economy', Dr Simon Longstaff and Victoria Whitaker of The Ethics Centre propose a core ethical framework. And although it is referring to the purpose of markets and corporations, I suggest it can also relate to us individually and collectively in our everyday personal and professional lives. The core ethical framework they propose is:

- **Respect people.**
- **Do no harm.**
- **Be responsible.**
- **Be transparent and honest.**[32]

I reckon that is a pretty good guide on what we need to consider before we make any decision or take any action.

When living in the light of day and applying the Light of Day Test to our decisions and actions, we can ask these four questions to help us decide if 'in the light of day' we ought to proceed with any decision or action.

1. If I make this decision or take this action, does it show my respect for those who might be impacted – does it show my respect for myself?

2. If I make this decision or take this action, will it harm others who might be impacted – will it harm me?

3. If I make this decision or take this action, am I willing to take responsibility for the consequences on others and/or on myself?

4. If I make this decision or take this action, am I prepared to be transparent to those who will be positively or negatively impacted – am I being honest – would others see me as being honest and transparent?

As I've mentioned previously, all of my academic and experiential research has led me to the conclusion that people will get your truth – over time your intentions, promises, actions, and results will either promote you as trustworthy or expose you as untrustworthy.

What has also become very clear to me is that trust impacts almost every measure of success in your personal and professional life, and when we talk about trust we also need to understand the impact of our intentions on trust.

Think back to our discussion so far on the Light of Day Test.

Being mindfully aware of your intentions, not only for yourself but how your decisions and actions will impact others, is fundamental to applying the Light of Day Test.

It adds depth to the words of Aristotle I shared in the first chapter: "Our actions and behaviours are our morals shown in conduct".

Our morals are those guiding principles upon which we live our lives, and our intentions reflect those morals.

Other people around you in your professional and personal life are constantly observing and determining your intentions, based on the decisions, actions and results you achieve … they're using their unconscious intelligence or intuition and weighing up your true intentions, based on your promises, actions and results.

They are weighing up whether they can trust you or not.

The new science of intention

As I continued my research into the importance of our intentions and the links between our intentions, trust and living a meaningful, flourishing, and prosperous life, I stumbled on a large amount of evidence-based research linking altruism with happiness and wellbeing.

Not wanting to spin off on an academic ramble over the various forms of altruism, let's keep it simple and go with psychologist Daniel Batson's definition of altruism, which is: "A motivational state with the ultimate goal of increasing another's welfare".[33]

So, the focus of altruism is to purposefully make life better for others in some way. But here is the really good news … being altruistic is not just good for others, it is also good for your own wellbeing.

In one study, for example, researcher Stephen Post found that when you have altruistic emotions and behaviours, you are most likely to also experience an increased sense of personal wellbeing, health, and longevity.[34]

This is backed up by Martin Seligman, the founder of the field of positive psychology. His research shows that the joy of undertaking an act of kindness provides profound satisfaction.[35]

You know how good and satisfied you are with yourself when you do a kind act … when you do some kind deed for no other reason than you wanted to make life better for someone else in some way.

Just today on my morning walk, a careless driver must have neglected to effectively tie down their load of tree and shrub cuttings and a rather large tied bundle of branches lay in the middle of the not-so-busy street.

I thought it just made sense to drag it off the road and onto the nature strip so cars could pass by without a concern.

I know … in the scheme of the more important altruistic acts the world needs now, this one small act of kindness might not be that significant. Nonetheless, I felt quite happy and proud that I had in this small way made life easier for others – and they would not even know what I had done.

You see, it was only one small act of kindness amidst what can often seem like insurmountable gloom and doom.

Consider these:

- **we've experienced a global pandemic**
- **we are experiencing ongoing and fast-paced digital disruption**
- **the debate continues over the impact of climate change**
- **there always seems to be political unrest between major nations**
- **people are reporting a greater sense of overwhelm stress and anxiety**
- **just driving to and from work we risk the potential of road rage**
- **there are constant reports of bullying both online and offline**
- **poverty and the gap between the haves and have-nots is reportedly rising**
- **the impact of discrimination by race, gender, sexual preference, age, ability/disability or other minority groups is always making news headlines.**

In all that gloom and doom, what the evidence-based research recommends is having a little more altruism in our approach to life might hold the key to managing and changing this world for the better.

Matthieu Ricard, Buddhist monk, philosopher, and best-selling author of *Altruism: The Science and Psychology of Kindness* agrees. He puts it this way:

"Altruism is not just a noble, somewhat naive ideal or a luxury only the affluent can afford. Now, more than ever, altruism is a necessity for the wellbeing of all".[36]

The more I researched this link between altruism and wellbeing, the more I realised what we're really talking about here is the impact a person's intention to do good for others can have, not only on the person toward whom the good intention is directed, but on the person with the good intention as well.

As a professional conference speaker and corporate educator, I am constantly looking for ways to apply evidence-based research from my fields of positive psychology and professional ethics to help organisational leaders create better experiences for their staff and customers.

This direction of my research around altruism led to me forming the following hypothesis:

When employees in workplace settings develop a positive (good) intention for their customers (and 'live up to' that positive intention), it will not only be good for the customers, but also for the employees, and ultimately for the organisation as well.

As a behavioural scientist, I decided to do my own 'at-work' experiment to test this hypothesis and collaborated with one of Australia's largest insurance organisations.

Just as was found with the other research I had encountered on the benefits of altruistic behaviour, employees who focused on what I now refer to as an *Applied Positive Intention*™ for their customers, and who over a three-week period reported on how they delivered on improving their customers' lives in some way, had a statistically positive increase in an important part of their overall sense of self-determination, as compared to a control group who were only focusing on task completion over the same period.[37]

Where this gets really interesting is a large series of research by Edward Deci and Richard Ryan, who I mentioned in chapter one. Their research highlights that people who have a high sense of ***self-determination*** in their professional and personal lives report higher levels of wellbeing and success across a range of measures.[38]

Deci's and Ryan's research shows that self-determined people are those who have a strong sense of autonomy (they have a sense of freedom of choice in how they go about doing what they do); they have a strong sense of competence (they believe they have the skills, knowledge, capacity, and access to resources to succeed in life); and they have a strong sense of relatedness (that they have caring, supporting, and positive relationships in their lives).

We will explore the topic of self-determination in more detail in chapter seven when we look into the significance of self-trust. But for now, we will continue to focus on just one of the elements of self-determination – that sense of relatedness (relationships) – because it is central to everything we are covering in this book.

And the evidence is clear: intentions matter because they impact our relationships with ourselves and others.

When you combine clarity of your intentions for yourself and for the people you impact in your various life roles, you establish your own foundation for living in the light of day and experiencing a meaningful, flourishing, and prosperous life based on intentional trust relationships.

Defining intention

Ok… so I have been harping on about just how important your intentions are, so let's take a moment here to get really clear on exactly what is meant by *intention.*

If you were to look up a dictionary meaning of the word you would find it is defined as 'a thing intended; an aim or a plan'. This is how most people would define intention – it is what we intend or mean to do. However, this definition is too narrow.

You might be familiar with the wonderful work of Simon Sinek and his TED talk[39] and book titled *Start With Why*. In brief, Sinek highlights that many organisations know *what* they're doing; some know *how* to get things done; and the really successful organisations are those whose people know *why* they do what they do – the positive impact they have on all stakeholders.[40]

However, long before Sinek's TED talk on *Start with Why*, way back in 1957, a British analytic philosopher, Elizabeth Anscombe, wrote a book titled *Intention*. [41]

It was in my reading of Anscombe's book during my Master's degree in Professional Ethics (it is one of the toughest books I have ever read), that I began to broaden my understanding and definition of intention.

Anscombe wrote: "An intention isn't just an understanding of WHAT one intends to do, but ought to carry with it an understanding of WHY one intends to do it".

So, both Anscombe and Sinek urge you to consider, *before any action*, not only what (and how) you are going to do it, but to also be clear about why you're going to do it.

This means you need to be clear about your reason, purpose, motivation, or drive to do what you intend to do.

In understanding *why* you intend to do *what* you intend to do, there is something else you need to also consider, and it is this additional element that makes all the difference to you being able to attract, build and maintain intentional trust relationships.

And this is where altruism and intention are linked.

The additional element you need to consider is the implication of your intention, not only for yourself, but the implications of your intended actions for others.

This now provides us with a more specific and useful definition of intention.

Your intention is a mindful awareness of *why* you are going to do *what* you are going to do and the *impact* it will have on others.

Let's explore these components of our definition of intention so that you can get to work and start creating your own *Applied Positive Intention* statements for the people you impact in your professional and personal life roles.

The mindful awareness of intention

Not everything you do in life will be intentional. However, your intentions will impact almost everything you do.

This highlights the importance of the first component of an intention – mindful awareness.

In much of the western world, mindfulness has become quite a fashionable topic for the past decade or so; however, its origins reach far back into the ancient practice of Buddhism.

Now, I need to be right up-front with you here. Despite having a Master of Science degree in Applied Positive Psychology, where I read volumes of overwhelming evidence-based research on the benefits of mindfulness meditation, it is just something I do not personally practise in the way that Buddhism teaches.

While I do attempt to still my mind and focus on my breathing as part of a regular and very basic daily yoga routine, I realise that technically it is a far cry from mindfulness meditation.

If you are a mindfulness meditation practitioner, and you're gaining all of the benefits to your physical and psychological wellbeing that the research highlights, understanding the importance of being more intentionally mindful in more moments that matter more often will just make sense to you. It is about being present.

If you are not a mindfulness meditation practitioner, the good news is that you can still gain a host of benefits to your professional and personal life through being mindfully aware of your intentions.

The process of writing out intention statements for the people you impact in your professional and personal life roles will help you to be more mindfully aware of your intentions.

This starts with gaining clarity of the *why* component of your intentions.

The *why* of intention

As our two sons were growing up, and they reached an age where both Liz and I were comfortable for them to venture out without us, before they would leave the house typically we'd give them a hug and say to them, "Make good decisions!"

Advising our sons to 'make good decisions' is of course based directly on the Light of Day Test, which to remind you once more is to ask yourself … 'Would I make this decision or take this action if they were held up in the light of day for all to see?'

When you think of the motives, reason or purpose behind your decisions and actions, you are gaining clarity of the *why* of your intentions.

Just as an aside, although our advice to our sons was to 'make good decisions', just as it is true for me and you, it didn't mean they always did.

The *what* of intention

Our definition of intention is a mindful awareness of why you are going to do what you are going to do and the impact it will have not only on you, but also on others.

So far, I have covered the first component – mindful awareness of *why*.

The *what* of intention in our definition is simply being clear on the actions we intend to implement.

My father was not an educated man. In fact, he left school when he was about 15 and started working with his father in the forest near our hometown as a sleeper cutter.

In case you are not familiar with what a sleeper cutter did, the thick planks of timber that railway tracks used to rest on were called 'sleepers'. My father, grandfather and great-grandfather all cut sleepers out of the red gum trees growing in the nearby Gunbower State Forest and sold them to the railways.

Although they were not educated men, they all had what I call 'simple wisdom'.

I am sure you know what I mean. Their wisdom might not have been academic, but it sure was practical, and often inescapably true.

Something Dad used to say that still sticks with me to this day is, "If you want to get stuff done … do stuff!"

That is pretty good, don't you think?

'If you want to get stuff done, do stuff.' It has become a bit of a mantra for me.

What I have learned over the years, however, is the importance of being clear about what stuff you are going to focus on.

This is where understanding and being mindfully aware of why you are going to do what you are going to do is so important. It helps you prioritise what you are going to do.

It is easy just to 'do stuff'. But doing the stuff that matters is what reaps you (and all of us) the real rewards of life.

While what you intend to do and why you intend to do it become clear, you'll also need to work out *how* you're going to do whatever it is you intend to do.

Sometimes, though – and you've more than likely already experienced this – the how won't always be clear ... but the more you focus on the why you intend to do what you intend to do, the how you might go about it will often become clearer.

I don't necessarily agree with my mentor, Jim Rohn, who is often quoted as saying "When the why is clear, the how is easy". Sometimes the how to achieve our goals isn't always clear (or easy), but I will agree that it becomes clearer the more we work on being mindfully aware of why we are going to do what we are going to do and the impact it will have on others.

This brings us to the final element of our definition of intention, which ties all the other elements together and really unlocks the power of intention.

The *impact* of intention

Being mindfully aware of the impact of your intentions *before you take action* says a lot about your character.

To act without any thought of the impact of the action is irresponsible and certainly risky – for yourself and for others who will be potentially impacted by your actions.

Remember the teaching of Aristotle that your actions and behaviours are your morals shown in conduct. Said another way, people will interpret your morals, your character and your intentions based on what they see you do … your actions.

To be mindfully aware of the impact of your intentions, not only to yourself, but the impact your actions will have on others *before you take the action* sets the foundation for trust.

For any relationship you have, over time, people will get your truth.

They will make an assessment of your truth, credibility, morals, and character by listening to your words and observing your actions ... they make an assessment of your intentions.

An intention to 'do stuff'

Earlier I shared my dad's advice: "If you want to get stuff done … do stuff".

While Dad certainly had no idea that I would be writing about that one day, he also had no idea that his advice to me all those years ago would form a key focus of scientific research around intention.

Having an intention is to have a mindful awareness of why you are going to do what you are going to do and the impact it will have, not only on you, but also on others.

It is important to also understand that within this definition it is the intention to implement, or 'do stuff' that will result in your intentions being fulfilled.

Research shows there is a significant difference between an intention to achieve a goal or result and an intention to do the work needed to achieve the goal or result.[42]

Psychologists refer to these different intentions as a ***goal intention*** and an ***implementation intention.***

A goal intention focuses on an end point or outcome. It is the intended result.

An implementation intention is a commitment to do what is required to achieve the result.

This is important because it highlights that an intention to achieve is not the same as an intention to take the action required to achieve a result.

This is certainly the case in education.

Intentions and deadlines

Think back to your school, college, or university experiences. You will have known other students who 'intended' to pass. They had a 'goal intention' but never followed through with an 'implementation intention' – to actually do the work required.

What difference does it make? That is what researchers Peter Gollwitzer and Veronika Brandstätter decided to find out.

In one study, college students were assigned a deadline to write a report within 48 hours of an event.

One group of students (experimental group) were coached on having a clear goal plus implementation intentions, whereas another group of students (the control group) were not.

Said another way, the experimental group were mindfully aware of *why* they wanted to achieve the goal and also clear on *what* they were promising themselves and their lecturer they were going to do.

Three-quarters of the experimental group of students with the clear goal and implementation intention met the deadline, compared with only one-third of the control group, who did not have implementation intentions.[43]

Intentions and health

Within our closest group of friends four women have been diagnosed with breast cancer and, thankfully, have all survived.

A 2015 report by a government body, Cancer Australia, titled 'Early Detection of Breast Cancer', states: "There is evidence that women can find breast changes due to early breast cancer".[44]

Seeking ways to increase the success rate of women completing regular breast self-examinations (BSE), a group of researchers led by Andrew Prestwich assigned one group (the experimental group) of women a goal intention plus implementation intention to undertake regular BSE.[45]

The control group were only assigned a goal intention to undertake regular BSE.

Of the experimental group, with both goal intention and implementation intention, a full 100 per cent completed regular BSE, compared with 53 per cent of the control group who had only a goal intention.

Intentions and exercise

In a further study, college students were assigned the task of regular vigorous exercise.[46]

Researchers established an experimental group with both goal and implementation intentions.

In this study the control group was instructed to focus on the potential for reduced risk of coronary heart disease as their motivation to complete the vigorous exercise, but without an implementation intention.

The students in the control group had an increase in their performance of vigorous exercise of between 29 and 39 per cent, which is impressive.

However, the students in the experimental group had an increase of 91 per cent in their performance of vigorous exercise.

Getting clear on the type of intention you have – especially for yourself – makes a big difference.

Intending to lose weight (goal intention) is not as likely to achieve a result as intending to exercise daily as a habit (implementation intention).

Clarity of intention increases meaning

While these examples from a much wider pool of research studies are compelling, there's potentially an even more important reason for you to embrace your intentions ... the impact that they can have on your sense of meaning in life.

Notice that I am referring to 'meaning in life' and not 'the meaning of life'.

This is an important distinction.

I referred earlier to a quote from Viktor Frankl. In his book *Man's Search for Meaning* Frankl explains this distinction eloquently by pointing out to us that it isn't so much the meaning of life that matters, but rather it is the "specific meaning of a person's life at a given moment".[47]

This highlights the importance of moving from the much bigger philosophical question around the meaning of life, to a more manageable and personal focus on finding or creating meaning in any given moment within your life.

My language around this is that by focusing on your intentions you become more intentionally mindful, in more moments that matter, more often, and this is what will help you bring more meaning into your personal and professional life.

Supporting Frankl's work in more recent times, positive psychology researchers like Michael Steger[48] and Roy Baumeister[49] have validated that our health and wellbeing are associated with the degree to which we have a sense of meaning in our personal and professional lives.

These and many other researchers have also found that one of the most reported sources from which people gain a sense of meaning in their life is their relationships.

This is why and how one of the real benefits of focusing on your intentions – what you want for others and not just what you want from them or for yourself – is a pathway to enhancing your sense of meaning in life, as suggested by Frankl, at any given moment.

Most of us don't consciously and regularly think about what makes life meaningful, and yet Roy Baumeister's research[50] reveals that, as humans, whether we realise it or not, we are all on a quest for a meaningful life and that this quest is based on four innate needs.

The first is the need for *purpose in our life*. This is about a sense that our actions and experiences today will lead toward either goal achievement or desired life fulfilment.

The second is the need for *values in our life*. This is about having a clear set of beliefs and guiding principles about right and wrong.

The third is the need for *self-efficacy*. This is about a belief that we have the capacity, competence, and resources to make a difference in the world in some way.

And the fourth is the need for *self-worth*. This is a belief that we are good and worthy of love and respect.

Here is an opportunity for you to complete a short self-assessment on each of these innate needs.

Take a moment and complete the questionnaire to consider whether there is an opportunity for you to work on one or more of these needs in your life by rating your answer to the questions below using the following scale:

1 = Very Low, 2 = Low, 3 = Medium,
4 = High, 5 = Very High

A meaningful life questionnaire

1. **Purpose in life:** To what extent do you believe your actions and experiences today are purposefully leading you toward achieving your goals and achieving a fulfilling life?

   1 2 3 4 5

2. **Values in life:** To what extent do you believe you have a clear set of beliefs and guiding principles about right and wrong in your life?

   1 2 3 4 5

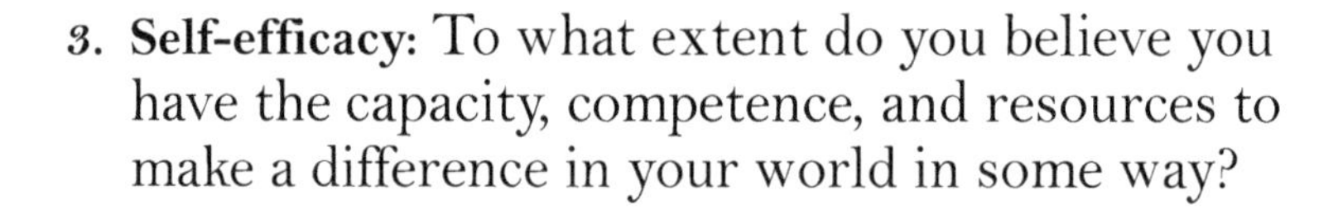

3. **Self-efficacy:** To what extent do you believe you have the capacity, competence, and resources to make a difference in your world in some way?

   1 2 3 4 5

4. **Self-worth:** To what extent do you believe that you are good and worthy of love and respect?

   1 2 3 4 5

My recommendation to you now that you have completed the exercise, is to pick just one area – purpose, values, self-efficacy, or self-worth – and ask this question:

What could I start, stop, or continue right now to help me be stronger in this area and help me strive to being the best version of myself?

We will explore ways for you to develop your purpose, values, self-efficacy, and self-worth in chapter seven on self-trust.

However, for now, know this: Living in the light of day is to experience a meaningful life and to live in ways where we take intentional action based on clear purpose, values, efficacy, and self-worth.

And it is through an understanding of the importance of your intentions for the people you impact through your various personal and work life roles that you establish the foundation to be able to live in the light of day and to live a meaningful life.

Ok … so that is a deep dive into intention, and my aim was to raise your awareness on why it is important for you, me, and everyone else to be clear about our intentions and to live more intentionally.

Now, let's move onto chapter four and provide you with a practical guide and process to help you do just that.

Chapter Three Summary

An Applied Positive Intention is a mindful awareness of why you are going to do what you are going to do and the impact it will have on others. By focusing on your positive intentions to make life better in some way for others in your professional and personal life, you become more intentionally mindful, in more moments that matter, more often, and this helps you to strive to be at your personal best, and to live a meaningful, flourishing, and prosperous life.

"Your purpose is not something you find;
it's how you live your life serving others."

Wayne W. Dyer

Chapter Four

Developing your intentions

My good friend Shawn Hunter is the author of *Small Acts of Leadership: 12 intentional behaviors that lead to big impact* (I highly recommend you read it), and among much wisdom he shares throughout the book, my favourite is a three-word sentence that I find to be just so powerful: "Action creates clarity".[51]

Here is how Shawn explains what he means:

"You can think and envision and ponder and predict what will or might happen when you start that new business, give that big presentation, run that marathon, or take that trip to Madagascar. But you won't know, really know, what it's like until you start. Experience is invaluable, and making tiny adjustments along the way is required, which is why action creates clarity."

I start with this wisdom from Shawn because this chapter is about taking action, and what I know is this: When you take action and complete the activities suggested in this chapter, you will gain clarity around what is really important in your life, your values and your relationships.

Having said that, though, what I also know is that it is easy to read about ideas, tips, suggestions and strategies in a book, and do nothing … even when there is scientific research to validate the value you will potentially gain by taking action.

This is also true when you have been provided with life-enhancing tips from a professional speaker at a conference, or even while listening to a radio interview.

I was being interviewed by Ian (Dicko) Dickson and Sarah Morice on their afternoon 2UE radio show in Sydney. They had invited me to talk about building trust and being more present in a fast-paced, technology-driven world.

I outlined a few tips and some of the evidence-based research that you have just read in the previous chapter, and I then suggested to Dicko and Sarah that one of the most powerful strategies to help with building trust and being present was to make a list of their life roles, identify the people they impact in those roles, and to then write out statements that reflected what they wanted *for* those people and not just what they wanted *from* them.

Sarah's immediate comment was, "Wow … I can see why that's so important – I focus on what I can do for others and how I can make a difference for them".

However, Dicko's follow-up comment was, "I dunno … it all sounds like a lot of hard work, time and effort".

My reply to Dicko was, "I agree … some of the simple things we can do to build trust relationships and be more present in a constantly distracting world are not always easy – but always worth the effort".

While I don't think I convinced Dicko, I am hopeful that Sarah might have put the strategy into action in some way.

What I hope for you is that you will follow Sarah's understanding of the value you can gain by being more intentional in your relationships and in your choices and actions to be living in the light of day, being the best version of yourself, and giving yourself the best opportunities to live a meaningful, flourishing, and prosperous life.

And that is what this chapter will help you do.

So, let's get down to work and provide you with this practical, easy, and yet powerfully positive process of developing Applied Positive Intention statements for the people you impact in your personal and professional life.

TASK ONE – IDENTIFY YOUR LIFE ROLES

This might seem a bit strange at first, but getting clear on the various life roles you have can be quite a revelation for many people, and when you mindfully accept the life roles you have, and get clear about the impact you have on others through your various roles, it can reap very positive rewards.

For example, one of my life roles is as a younger brother to my older brother, Chris.

We are two very different people and have not always had the best of relationships, and there was often quite a bit of friction between us.

We are brothers, not friends.

You might find it odd for me to say this, but if we were not brothers, we certainly would not be friends ... we just see the world in very different ways. If we were not brothers, we would not have a relationship – there would be no reason for one.

However, we *are* brothers, and it took me many years to understand that if I didn't 'play my younger-brother role in life' whenever in conversation with Chris, our relationship became unclear, and that's what was causing the friction.

This is not to say a brother or sister can't also be your friend. Of course, they can. However, it isn't always the case.

I am now clear and comfortable in my role as younger brother to Chris. I know what I want for him to experience through our relationship, and I work hard on living up to that; and our relationship, while far from perfect, is one of (mainly) mutual respect.

So, the first task in developing your Applied Positive Intention statement is to understand that you have various life roles. Take a moment now to think about and make note of them.

You might be a parent, a husband/wife/partner, a sibling, a son or daughter, a brother or sister, a friend.

Your professional life roles could include that you are a leader, coach, colleague, team member, salesperson, or service provider.

TASK TWO – WHO IS IMPACTED

The second task is to think about who you impact through each of those life roles.

For example, one of my life roles is as a husband, and it is pretty obvious that in that role I will impact my wife Liz's life.

However, and even though there is obvious overlap with other life roles (including son-in-law, father and friend), the other people I impact through this role as a husband include Liz's parents, Liz's siblings and their children, and of course our own two sons as well.

Returning to my earlier example of my life role as younger brother to Chris. Aside from the obvious impact my relationship with Chris will have on the two of us, there's also the impact the relationship will have on Chris' wife, their children, our father, and on my wife Liz and our sons when they're in situations when we are all together.

Now there is the chance that you might skip over this. It does take a bit of time and courage, but the process highlights and makes very real the impact you have on others through your various life roles.

My advice is to break this down to the life roles that matter most to you at this moment of your life and leave the others for another time when they might become more important, for whatever reason.

TASK THREE – APPLIED POSITIVE INTENTION STATEMENT

The third task, now that you have identified each life role and the various people you impact through it, is to develop an Applied Positive Intention statement for each of those people or groups of people.

For example, if one of your life roles was as a business owner, rather than individually listing every customer you have, you might group them under the heading 'customers' or 'clients'.

Developing an Applied Positive Intention statement is a process of completing a statement that starts with: "My intention for (this person or group of people) is…" and then writing what it is you want *for* that person or group of people and to ensure you're not just focusing on what you want *from* them.

As you are applying this, think about what you want them to have, to feel or to experience.

Now instead of the word 'intention' you could use alternatives like goal, wish or hope, and that's fine, so long as you maintain your focus on the full definition of what an intention is – a mindful awareness of *why* you are going to do *what* you are going to do and the impact it will have, not only on you, but also on others.

Here are some examples to get you started:

- **If you are in sales, what is your intention, wish or hope for your customers/clients?**

- **If you are in a personal relationship, what is your intention, wish or hope for your partner?**

- **If you are in a job role where you rely on others and they rely on you, what is your intention, wish or hope for your work colleagues?**

- **If you are a parent, what is your intention, wish or hope for your child?**

- **If you are a leader, what is your intention, wish or hope for your team?**

- **If you are in business and you have suppliers or referral partners, what is your intention, wish or hope for them?**

As you're writing out your intention statements, continually ask yourself if this intention is what that person or group would genuinely want for themselves ... is this what they would hope you intended for them?

This leads into the fourth and final task of developing your Applied Positive Intention statements, which is to check with the person or group that what you intend is what they would want.

Here I recommend you share your intention statement with the other person, using the Four-Step Intention-Agreement Process:

1. Start with your focus on the relationship.

2. Let them know you have been thinking about them.

3. State your intention.

4. Check that they agree.

The conversations you have might look something like:

(1) Start with your focus on the relationship:

"I've been thinking about us lately..." or
"I've been thinking about our relationship lately..." or
"I've been thinking about you lately..." or
"I've been thinking about your business lately...".

(2) Then, let them know what it is that you have been thinking about them, by saying something like:

"and I just want to check in with you on how I'm doing with us" or
"and I've been thinking about what I'm contributing to your business" or
"and I've been thinking about what I want for you, not what I want from you".

(3) Next, state your intention by saying something like:

"and it became clear to me that what I hope for you is...
(and share your Applied Positive Intention statement).

(4) Now, check that they agree by asking something like:

"So, I just wanted to check, does that make sense to you?" or

> "I just wanted to make sure that's what you want for you too?" or
>
> "I wanted to check that I'm on the right track and that's what you're wanting us to help you achieve in your business?"

In these examples I have tried to provide you with enough variations on how the conversation might be structured, without wanting to provide you with a script.

You need to work out how you would check with the person or group, that what you intend for them – what you wish, want or hope for them – is what they want for themselves, and that they would welcome you helping them experience it.

Developing your Applied Positive Intention statement for the people you impact in your various life roles is important. It sets the foundation for an intentional, trust-based relationship.

However, please do not overlook the importance of ensuring that what you intend for others is what they want for themselves.

Otherwise, despite wanting to deliver on your best intentions for them, any promises, actions and results you might achieve in delivering on that intention may not be of meaningful value to the other person or group.

The paradox of personal intention

Most of what I have covered so far on intention surrounds the importance of focusing on your intention for the people you impact in your life roles.

Paradoxically, in order to be able to focus and deliver on your intentions for others, it is of paramount importance that you take care of yourself … that you are clear on your intentions for you.

Taking care of yourself is based around self-trust and, unfortunately, this is a life role many people neglect. In chapter seven we will delve into the importance of self-trust in more detail; however, for now, setting the platform or foundation for self-trust starts with you being very clear about your intention for yourself.

So, take this opportunity to write out an Applied Positive Intention statement for yourself by completing the following statement:

"In my life role of taking care of me, my intention is…"

As you consider the question *'What is your intention, wish or hope for you?'*, you will quickly realise that much of your intention will be within your own control to deliver on.

However, it will also become clear, at times, that to deliver on your intentions for yourself you will need the help of others.

This brings up the importance of having the courage and collaboration skills to trust others, which is the topic of discussion in chapter eight.

Richard's moment of intentional truth

Let me share with you a wonderful moment of intentional truth for a financial adviser in one of my programs.

We had just completed an activity where the audience members shared with three other people their Applied Positive Intention statement for their clients and I asked for volunteers to share with the rest of the audience what they had discovered from the activity.

Richard raised his hand. He was a slightly greying man, aged in his early 50s. The roaming microphone was handed to him by a member of the conference support team and we could all hear him take a deep breath in and a shaky breath out. He looked directly at me and here is what he said:

"David, I've been a financial planner now for the best part of nearly thirty years, and before I came to the conference today …" he paused, looked around the room, took another deep breath in and out and continued, "before I came to the conference today, I was seriously thinking it was time to quit".

You could hear a pin drop in the audience because they got Richard's truth. You could also sense the supportive energy in the room as we all waited to hear what Richard had to say next:

"But that exercise of writing out and sharing what my intention is for my clients, reminded me of why I first became a financial planner".

When Richard spoke this time, you could see his body language start to become more positive.

"You see, I became a financial planner because I saw it as a noble profession and an opportunity to really make a positive difference to people's lives. But over the past decade, as the demands of compliance, administrative work, technology, and a bunch of other demands have consumed me … I felt overwhelmed, and I had forgotten about the most important reason behind what I do. I never called it my intention because I didn't really have a word for it, other than that I knew the advice I provided my clients really did make a positive difference."

Richard paused again, and you could see he was visibly moved.

He turned to face the audience members – his colleagues in the financial planning industry – and said, "My intention, my wish, my hope for my clients is to help every one of them to be financially secure so that they can live the best life they possibly can. And I'm ready again to be the best financial planner I can be and to be the financial planner they need me to be".

Richard sat down to a heartfelt, lengthy round of applause from his colleagues, who certainly got his truth.

Many audience members may have learned a similar lesson through the activity and had begun to take stock of their own truth and define their intentions.

I received a personal email from Richard a few weeks later, thanking me for my presentation and telling me about his new-found energy.

Since that day, so many things in his office had started to change for the better.

While he was still completing all the administrative and compliance tasks required of him, his focus now was on how completing these tasks would benefit his clients and allow him to do a better job for them.

He was thoroughly enjoying meeting his existing clients and restating his intention for them. He was thrilled that their typical response was, "We know that, Richard; that's why you're our financial planner".

He also noticed his renewed client focus and intention rubbing off on others in the office. It was not just affecting him and his clients; it was positively affecting the office culture.

Toward the end of his email, Richard also shared the following:

"David, during a first appointment with a prospective husband and wife client, early in our conversation I decided to state my intention to them, just like I had written down at the conference. I am convinced it was this genuine truth, of me letting them know why I was so proud of being a financial planner, which led them to agree to become a new client of mine. Thank you for reconnecting me with my truth".

Richard is just one of many examples of my clients who have come to understand the micro and macro impact of their intention, and what it means to be living in the light of day.

And just as so many of my clients have experienced, once you align yourself with positive intentions for people you impact in your various life roles, you will start to see immediate and positive changes in yourself and in the people you impact in those life roles.

You will become happier with who you are and find meaning in what you have and in what you do – you will be living in the light of day and experiencing a more meaningful, flourishing, and prosperous life.

Tuning into intention – being truly present

Understanding the importance of intention can help you to really tune in and be present when it matters most – when you are about to communicate in some way with others.

If you're about to make a phone call, send an email, go into a client meeting, share an idea in a team meeting, meet a friend to catch up over coffee, or sit down to dinner with your family, it will only take a few seconds to stop and ask yourself, "What is my intention here?"

Watch how magic happens when you do. Notice the impact this simple but powerful process has, not only on you, but watch what happens for those around you.

And even if it feels a bit strange at first to do this, know that because this is your genuine intention to do your best for the people you impact, having that 'higher purpose' – a focus to genuinely make a positive difference to others

– influences how your actions are delivered and perceived … people will get your truth.

Get your intentions clear and earning, building, and maintaining trust in your life becomes easier.

As I have highlighted in this chapter, science validates the importance of having clarity of intention.

Clear intentions for others increase your sense of meaning in life, and also increase your capacity for success in your personal and professional life. You are now able to make intentional promises and commitments to the people you impact through your various life roles.

If you're not making intentional promises and commitments, the potential is that you will be leaving it up to others to arrive at unintentional expectations you will find it difficult to manage and live up to.

Summary on intention

Wow … I referred you to a quote from Jim Rohn and warned you that this was going to be a deep dive into the true meaning of your intentions and how they can impact you and others professionally and personally.

You've read how your intentions impact:

- **your trustworthiness**
- **your sense of wellbeing**
- **your relationships**
- **your sense of meaning**

- **your self-determination**

- **your goal achievement**

… and the list goes on and on.

I hope by now you have no doubt and agree with me that *intentions matter!*

So now I recommend you take a break and just let your mind rest for a while, and when you're ready, come back refreshed and ready to learn how the ***Intentional Steps to Trust*** process will help you live in the light of day, help you strive to be at your best, and experience a meaningful, flourishing, and prosperous life.

Chapter Four Summary

An Applied Positive Intention Statement is a statement that clearly articulates what you want FOR other people, not just what you want from them. When you take action to live up to your positive intentions to make life better for others in your personal and business life, you will find this intentional life habit will impact your trustworthiness, your sense of wellbeing, your relationships, your sense of meaning, your self-determination, and your goal achievement.

"The best way to find out if you can trust somebody is to trust them."

Ernest Hemingway

Chapter Five

A fresh look at trust

Imagine what your world would be like if no one could be trusted ... not even yourself.

What if you could not trust your husband, wife, partner, family members or friends, and what if they did not trust you?

How would the commercial world function without trust?

What if iconic global brands like Apple, Johnson & Johnson and IKEA struggled to build loyal customers and the organisational leaders were all viewed as untrustworthy by their employees?

What if you could not trust any sales or customer service people ... how would you decide on what product or service to buy?

Who would you turn to if you could not trust your butcher, hairdresser, or your doctor?

How safe would your country be if the distrust between hostile nations extended to leaders of allied countries not trusting each other?

You see ... a world without trust would quite simply be chaotic; and yet, when you consider statistics like 59 per cent of us globally are just not sure what is true or not anymore,[52] the fear of 'fake news' is a clear sign that we are living in a world where trust is at risk.

If you were to ask most business leaders whether they have a 'trust issue', the majority would answer no. However, global research by Ernst and Young found that less than half of full-time workers say they have 'a great deal of trust' in their employers, their bosses, and their work colleagues.[53]

Put simply, at least half of us are finding it hard to trust anyone – at least in the workplace.

Beyond the workplace and in our private lives, as pointed out earlier, we are finding it increasingly hard to trust once well-trusted brands. It seems almost daily now that another company is 'caught out' breaching the trust of their customers, or their employees, or their shareholders, or their suppliers, or the broader community.

In a wonderfully written article by Amanda Hooton in the *Sydney Morning Herald*, titled 'Other people's money', she poses this question: "What exactly is it that compels good people to do bad things?"[54]

It is a great question, isn't it.

Hooton extends the question to being about people "who have so neatly managed to ignore the most basic principles of right and wrong, good and bad, decency and immorality".

But again, what causes good people to make bad decisions?

This is a question Mike Erwin, CEO of the Character & Leadership Center, explored as part of his research for the book *Lead Yourself First*, which he co-authored with Raymond Kethledge.[55]

Erwin suggests there are six reasons that might cause any of us to make bad decisions:

1. Decision fatigue – when we've been constantly under pressure to make lots of decisions.

2. Distraction – information and communication overload.

3. Lack of input – when we just don't feel like we are able to contribute.

4. Multi-tasking – trying to do too many things at once (see decision fatigue and distraction).

5. Emotions – getting hooked into difficult thoughts and feelings that blind us to the facts.

6. Analysis paralysis – with so much information at our fingertips, we can over analyse everything to the point of not making decisions – which can be ineffective as well.[56]

Most of us could probably admit to experiencing at least two of these six causes of bad decisions on any given day of our lives, and I'm sure you can imagine that if that's true for you, it's true for most of us – so we all have the potential to make bad or poor decisions … decisions that can breach trust and negatively impact ourselves and others.

So, the fast-paced world most of us live in can put trust at risk, which puts relationships at risk and puts our potential to be the best versions of ourselves at risk and our potential to flourish in life at risk.

This is what social commentators, academic researchers and philosophers have long been suggesting – when trust is at risk, our functional effectiveness as humankind to flourish is at risk.

Rachel Botsman summed this up well in her book, *Who Can You Trust?,*[57] when she wrote, "Without trust, and without an understanding of how it is built, managed, lost and repaired, a society cannot survive and it certainly cannot thrive".

This chapter will provide you with a fresh look and understanding of trust, and then help you avoid making bad decisions. It will guide you on how to earn, build and maintain trust relationships, which will help you be the best version of yourself: to live a good life ... to live a more meaningful, flourishing, and prosperous life.

I know you already get the importance of trust in your life, and while it's a bit of a truism to say 'trust matters', it's important to dig a little deeper into what it is, why it matters, and just how often it matters.

Trust is woven through the fabric of our daily lives in so many ways, and often we are not even aware of where we have automatically placed our trust.

Trust and everyday habits

When we wake in the morning, we automatically trust the quality and safety of the toothpaste we brush our teeth with, as well as the soap we use and the shampoo.

Most of us don't even bother to consider what the ingredients are, where they were sourced, how ethical (or legal) the manufacturer's operation is, or how they treat their workers.

Trust in news

Many of us automatically trust the news we hear, watch, read or engage with on whatever mainstream or social media platform we choose.

According to the Pew Research Center[58] around 68 per cent of people surveyed report that they primarily use social media as their number one source of news.

What is interesting here, though, is that their research also suggests 58 per cent of that same group believe the news on social media was likely to be "largely inaccurate".

So, many of us are switching to social media as our prime source of news, despite the fact that we are a bit wary of whether the news we are watching is real or fake.

Another problem here is that social media platforms use algorithms to determine what it is you value, like, believe and are most interested in ... and those algorithms then send mostly only what supports your beliefs and values.

That means more and more people are limiting their perspectives to just reinforce their own points of view, assumptions, and beliefs. At the same time, they are limiting their potential to see the world through other points of view. All of which puts truth, empathy, and trust at risk.

Sure, I realise of course that there is also the argument that mainstream TV and radio reporting can 'pick a side' and report biased news too. The point I am making here is that many of us just automatically trust the news we receive (or at the very least are influenced by it) from whichever source we consume it.

Trust in cars

We automatically trust that the car we drive will get us to our destination safely.

And yet, as reported in the New York Times, upward of 42 million vehicles had faulty airbags installed, placing drivers and their passengers at risk of injury or death.[59]

Trust at work

When we arrive at work we automatically trust (most of) our colleagues to help us achieve our work tasks, our manager to support us, and our executive leadership team to be making and implementing strategic and operational decisions that are in the best interest of all stakeholders (and not just shareholders).

Well, maybe this is an area where many of us do not 'automatically' place our trust. Certainly, that's what the Edelman research on trust outlined earlier is telling us – trust in institutions and leadership is in decline and has moved more into a culture of distrust.

Trust in food

We automatically trust that the coffee we drink during our work breaks and the food we buy for lunch is safe for us to eat and drink.

Many of us are blessed with fresh food and high-quality food preparation standards. In Australia it is estimated that 4.1 million people experience food poisoning annually.[60] In the U.S. the Center for Disease Control and Prevention (CDC) estimates the figure is closer to 48 million,[61] and the Food Standards Agency in the U.K. estimate around 2.4 million cases of foodborne disease annually.[62]

Trust in relationships

I am blessed with and so very grateful for the relationship I have with my wife, Liz, and we certainly trust each other, and we value each other's trust.

Apparently, however, that is not the case for many Australians.

McCrindle research group report that one in three marriages in Australia end in divorce. Perhaps, on a more positive note (sort of), they also report that those marriages that do end in divorce are at least lasting longer than they did two decades ago.[63] In the U.S. while divorce rates have fallen since 2009, the average length of marriage is reported as just 8 years.[64] According to the U.K. Office for National Statistics, in 2020 the average duration of marriage as 11.9 years.

These examples of where many of us place our trust automatically in our everyday lives highlight just how important trust is to our very existence.

They also highlight how this automatic placement of trust can be misplaced, questioned, and breached … and sometimes with disastrous results.

Taking trust for granted

So, trust is undeniably a core part of our life, and sometimes automatic trust can be misplaced.

But there is another problem with this automatic placement of trust.

As I have written earlier, I think it's fair to say that most of us 'get' that trust is important ... but that's the problem.

When we just 'get' things, or just 'accept' things, this is what creates our automatic, and mindless, response to things.

We as humans have this amazing capacity to get used to things. It is core to our existence. And that is a good thing, because the one constant in our lives is change – always has been, always will be.

While change is not always easy, and sometimes unwanted, the reality is, change or disruption is the natural state of human existence.

We as humans have this innate drive to improve, which means we are driven to change the status quo in that pursuit of a better life, a better world.

While in the early stages of change some of us may feel overwhelmed, the majority get used to the new changes in our world and return to a sense of stability – at least until the next change occurs.

I refer to this as the IUTI syndrome, which stand for 'I'm Used To It'.

Let me take a moment here to share with you an example of the IUTI syndrome, and I'm sure you'll be able to think of similar examples in your own life.

Geoff is one of our good friends and he is a bit of an early adopter when it comes to new technology. Before flat-screen televisions became a standard household item, Geoff was one of the first of our friends to purchase one ... and he didn't hold back – he bought the biggest flat-screen TV on the market – and it cost a lot of money.

A few of us went around to his place to check it out and watch the football game on his brand-new TV.

We were impressed and said so to Geoff. He was pretty chuffed and proud, saying, "It's very impressive isn't it".

About a month later it was football finals time and a few of us returned to Geoff's place to watch the final on his big TV.

While we all told Geoff again just how impressed we were, he kind of shrugged his shoulders and said, "You know ... I'm getting kind of used to it now".

That is the IUTI syndrome in action.

Geoff had become 'used to' his new TV ... and in shrugging his shoulders, and in his tone of voice, you could tell that the sparkle, newness, and impressiveness of the TV had diminished.

In other words, he was just taking it for granted now, and in doing so he was devaluing it.

While we were still in awe, Geoff had just got used to it and the IUTI syndrome had reduced the joy he was getting out of the TV.

This is true for us when we get a new car, move into a new house, or have any change in our lives. It doesn't take to long for the IUTI syndrome to kick in and all of a sudden that amazing feeling of the new car or new whatever diminishes, and we just start taking it for granted.

Another example is how quickly we can get used to a beautiful view – maybe you are lucky enough to have a beautiful view from your home or maybe your office? It doesn't take too long and you start to forget the view is even there – you just get used to it, and ignore it … until someone new sees it for the first time and reminds you just how lovely it is. While you might respond to that person with an acknowledgment, it won't take long before you just get used to it again and ignore it like you'd been doing before you were reminded of just how lovely it is.

The IUTI syndrome and trust

So, what has all this IUTI syndrome got to do with trust? I am glad you asked.

Just as we can quickly become used to 'things' in our lives, the IUTI syndrome can also apply to relationships.

It is very easy for us to just get used to the relationships we have in our lives – with our partner, family, friends, work colleagues, and customers.

When we just get used to relationships, we unintentionally start to take them for granted. And then we devalue them – the very things that are the most important in our lives.

When we devalue relationships, we put *trust* at risk … which means that almost everything in our lives is at risk.

Trust in a new and disruptive world

Our capacity to trust automatically is becoming even more apparent in the fast-paced digital world.

It was not so long ago that if you asked anyone would they buy anything 'online' they'd roll their eyes and say, "No".

That is certainly not the case anymore.

In fact, according to a McKinsey report on the effects of online purchases since the Covid-19 pandemic, more people expect to make more purchases online than before the pandemic.[65] That number of online buyers is estimated by Statista.com to be over 2 billion people.[66]

All this increased trust in online shopping does not come without a cost.

While the number of us who are more trusting of our online purchasing is increasing, so too are the scams that are catching out an increasing number of 'trusting' people.

The U.S. Federal Trade Commission estimates in 2020 online shoppers lost more than $246million and in Australia, around $7.4million had been reported as being lost through online shopping scams.[67]

Beyond our online shopping, our capacity to trust strangers seems to be spreading further into our lives.

A recent PWC research paper titled 'The Sharing Economy' gives this insight into just how far our capacity to trust strangers seems to be spreading in our lives.

"Around the world, a new wave of peer-to-peer, access-driven businesses is shaking up established categories. Whether borrowing goods, renting homes, or serving up micro-skills in exchange for access or money, consumers are showing a robust appetite for the sharing-based economy."[68]

One of the iconic success stories of this new economy and marketplace is of course Airbnb.

Airbnb report that their "accommodation marketplace provides access to 5+ million unique places to stay in more than 81,000 cities and 191 countries".[69]

People are willing to trust and 'share' their homes or rooms with strangers, for a price.

However, sometimes that trust is misplaced.

According to an online survey of over 1000 Airbnb guests and 100 hosts conducted by House Method, nearly half of the hosts had considered quitting Airbnb and more than a fifth report that they have taken down their listings as a result of negative guest behaviour.[70]

The other icon of the sharing economy is Uber.

Out of consumer distrust, disappointment and finally disengagement with the taxi industry, Uber emerged as the trustworthy alternative to those hard-to-find-taxis-when-you-needed-them-most.

Talk about automatically trusting ... we have now moved into a new world of people trusting strangers who have no other qualification than a driver's licence.

As a sidebar here about Uber and trust, at the time of writing this book, globally Uber is under attack from an increasing number of new ride-sharing companies, including Lyft in the USA, Bolt in Europe, Yandex in Russia, DiDi in China and Ola in Australia.

In a *Forbes* article by Stephen McBride, he points out, "Uber customers don't care about Uber" and that most Uber customers would switch if it cost more for an Uber than a ride with a competitor.[71]

A 2019 *Washington Post* article highlights "Uber has a reputation problem" that stemmed from a range of scandals, including internal cultural issues, price gouging, and driver assault charges.[72]

So, the trustworthy alternative to the taxi industry has shown the costs of distrust with, their competition taking more and more market share.

I won't try to predict the future success or failure of Uber, but the costs of distrust from a damaged reputation are obviously not looking too positive and, returning to McBride's *Forbes* article, he writes this about Uber's future: "Let me say this one more time: It's a race to the bottom".

Yes, the sharing economy has opened opportunities for many disruptors to launch new businesses in existing markets and create new markets. But make no mistake, over time the novelty of the newness of the sharing economy is lost and people are still looking for businesses they can trust.

So whether it's Uber, one of its competitors, Airbnb or one of the other sharing economy businesses – such as Boataffair.com that offers boutique boat rentals, DesksNearMe.com that rents out office space, Lendingclub.com that offers peer-to-peer lending, Getaround.com that allows you to use other people's cars when they don't need them, or Taskrabbit.com to connect you with someone who's handy with stuff you're not – all of these and many other emerging sharing economy businesses need to focus on doing things in ways that earn, build and maintain the trust of their customers.

Who's rating who?

The opportunities for individuals to share their assets, skills or knowledge are certainly opening with this new sharing economy, and what's emerged is a major shift in the way a service purchase and experience is rated, not just in the sharing economy, but in traditional businesses and services as well.

In the traditional market economy, all the emphasis of whether you could trust a company, supplier or salesperson was based on consumer feedback.

While this rating of providers remains in the sharing economy, the big shift is now that consumers of the service are also rated by the suppliers on their trustworthiness.

The upside of this new way of reporting online through rating systems on who we can trust is that we can weigh up other people's experiences and advice from both the seller and buyer perspectives.

The downside is that one mistake, or even someone having a bad day, might result in a 'poor rating' that could impact the perceived trustworthiness of someone, and significantly impact their lifestyle choices in the future.

This dual rating of a service experience does demonstrate the importance of how trust must be considered in terms of the trustworthiness of all parties involved in the relationship, or in this case the transaction.

So, we now exist in a traditional marketplace as well as this once emerging, and now established, sharing economy, and in both cases the evidence is clear that trust is the driving force for success.

This view is summed up best in this statement from a recent report by PWC that found innovation and agility are core drivers of any organisation's success, but that *trust* will be the key driver of success over the next decade. [73]

"A lack of trust is directly damaging for economic growth ... and for a company's success, holding back investments, entrepreneurship and innovation."

But what is trust?

We have explored how trust impacts almost every moment in our lives and how often (not always) we are automatically trusting, without really thinking about it.

I would like to pose an important question to you now: What does it mean when you 'trust' someone?

For the past 25 years I have been asking that question and collecting responses from thousands of audience members at corporate conferences.

As part of the research for this book, I decided to unscientifically also ask some of my high school buddies who are part of my favourite Facebook Group (and in reality, one of the only reasons I'm on Facebook). Here are some of their unedited responses.

"When you trust someone, you know they will always have your back. Also, you can tell them anything and it won't go any further."

"When you trust someone, you feel you can rely on them."

"When you trust someone, you don't really know if you can rely on them until a crisis happens."

"When you trust someone, it's having faith in the best outcome, whether from a person or a situation."

"When you trust someone in your personal life, it's being sure that they will maintain your privacy, keep your secrets and act in your best interests. In professional life it's that they will give their honest opinion, privately warn you when they think you may be making a mistake and giving credit where credit is due."

"When you trust someone, it means never to doubt."

"When you trust someone, it means that they will act in my best interest, in an honest, respectful and caring manner."

"When you trust someone, there is no doubt in my mind, I don't second guess them."

"When you trust someone, it means having friends and family that I would put my life and the life of my children in their hands. In a work sense trust is about people acting with integrity, upholding the organisation's values, and being focussed on the best outcomes for clients. Looking after team members."

So, how close are these responses to how you would answer the question?

Aside from my high school buddies (some of whom are in the corporate world), one of the consistent responses I get from conference audience members is this:

"I'm not sure … I just trust them."

Trust seems to mean different things to different people, and not just my school buddies and conference audience members.

Why?

We each see trust based on our own unique experiences and perspectives.

Psychologists tend to view trust from the perspective of a personal trait an individual possesses … we are either a trusting type of person or we are not. Sociologists tend to see trust as part of our social structure … without trust, society does not function effectively, caringly, humanely. And economists tend to view trust as a choice mechanism … it is a choice we make to take a risk that the person who we are trusting will live up to our expectations.[74]

In addition, when you contextually think about trust, it can be used as a noun (for example, the formation of a 'family trust' for accounting purposes); as a verb (for example, *'I will trust you'* – the 'act' of trusting); or as an adjective (for example, *'She is trustworthy'* – the 'description' of trust).

Simplifying the complex

So, trust is a lot more complex than just 'a feeling' or something we do, and we could certainly go down a theoretical rabbit hole trying to define what many researchers have resolved to being quite difficult, because of the contextual differences we can have when we talk about trust.

Most of us, however, do not live in an academic world where we've got the time or inclination to over-think this vast range of perspectives on how to define trust.

For that reason, I am going to suggest we start with the *Oxford Dictionary* definition, which is:

"Trust is a firm belief in the reliability, truth, or ability of someone or something".[75]

However, I am going to suggest we slightly change and expand it to this:

Trust is a firm belief in the truth, ability or reliability of someone or something to deliver an expected result or outcome.

I have purposely changed the order of the word's truth, ability and reliability for reasons that will become clear when we discuss trustworthiness in chapter six.

Based on this latter definition, when we trust it means we've got this belief, feeling, knowledge, awareness, or maybe even hope, that a person (or in some cases, a material object) can be relied on, that they are truthful, and that they have the ability to do whatever it is we expect and rely upon them to do.

Recall the quote from Aristotle I introduced you to earlier in this book, that our actions and behaviours are our morals shown in conduct – or our trustworthiness shown in conduct.

You will recall my language around this is that people will get your truth and that over time your intentions, promises, actions and results will either promote you as trustworthy, or expose you as not.

Let me now introduce you to the Intentional Steps to Trust process.

This process is a practical and very workable way to not only better understand what it means to trust and to be trustworthy, but also to help you practically do things that will lead to you living in the light of day. It will allow you to earn, build and maintain trust, so that you can live an even more meaningful, flourishing, and prosperous life.

Let's now dig a little deeper into each of the steps.

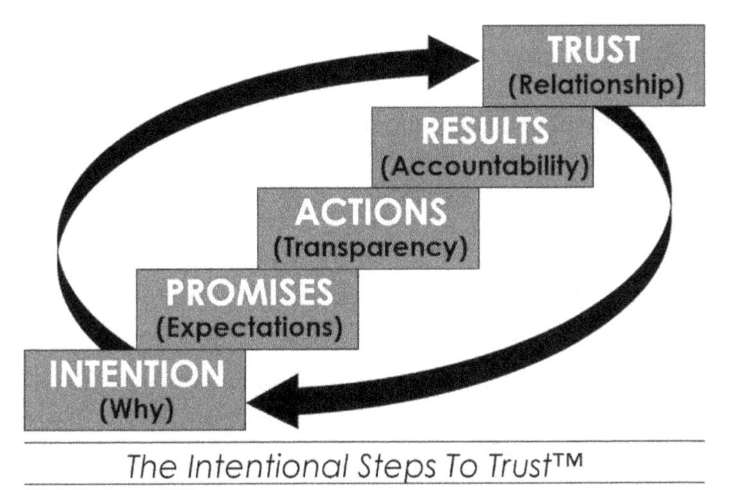

The Intentional Steps To Trust™

People Will Get Your Truth! *Over time your intentions, promises, actions and results will either promote you as trustworthy or expose you as not.*

Intention – the first step in the Intentional Steps to Trust

In chapters three and four we covered the importance of getting your intention clear, and it is the first step in the Intentional Steps to Trust.

Whatever the relationship, whether it's your relationship with yourself, or with another person or a group of people, starting with a clear and positive intention to make life better for you, the other person or group is the first step to living in the light of day and, of course, in building intentional trust.

You start with intention by applying the simple yet powerful process of writing out an Applied Positive Intention Statement – a statement that clearly identifies what you want *for* someone and not just focusing on what you want from them.

When you're clear about it, this clarity of having a positive intention to make life better for someone will become evident to the other person – that you have their best interests as your guiding motivation.

Again, Aristotle said, "Our actions and behaviours are our morals shown in conduct".

What I'm suggesting to you is that we can interplay the word 'morals' with 'intentions' and say our intentions become evident (shown in conduct) to others through our actions and behaviour.

If you're not clear about your intentions, then your actions and behaviours are left to chance – this is when unintentional actions and behaviours can lead to unintentional results that negatively impact others … trust and relationships are put at risk.

You can see in the Intentional Steps to Trust model that, along with the first step being intention, I've also included the word *Why*.

In chapters three and four we also did a deep dive into the full meaning of intention – that it's a mindful awareness of why you are going to do what you are going to do and the impact it will have on others.

So while your intentions are far more than just understanding why you're going to do whatever it is you intend to do, being aware of what is motivating you (your why) to make a decision or take an action is so important.

Purpose – meaning in life and intention

Now, I don't know if this is true for you, but if I were to ask most people, "What's your purpose in life?" the majority would find that question difficult to answer.

There are very few people who have a strong sense of a 'life purpose' or 'calling'.

You might think of people like Gandhi, Mother Teresa, or Nelson Mandela. You might personally know some people who do have a life purpose or calling (maybe even yourself). They are so clear about what they want to achieve, and they are so motivated and driven to achieve it, almost nothing will get in their way of staying true to their purpose in life.

Motivational self-help gurus across the globe preach from conference stages the importance for us all to find our purpose in life.

However, the evidence-based research on that advice suggests it might not always be such a good thing.

One of the leading researchers in the field of purpose and meaning in life is Michael Steger, who suggests that people experience the presence of meaning in life when they "comprehend themselves and the world, understand their unique fit in the world, and identify what they are trying to accomplish in their lives".[76]

According to Steger's and others' research,[77] people who have a sense of meaning and purpose in their lives also tend to report a strong and positive sense of psychological wellbeing and flourishing in their lives.

So, that is certainly aligned with what the motivational gurus tell us – having a purpose and sense of meaning in life is good for us … if we have it.

But what if we don't? This is where the research becomes interesting.

It seems that searching for a purpose or meaning in life does not mean we will ever necessarily find it and, in contrast to what the motivational gurus tell us, the evidence-based research shows that searching for meaning or purpose in life is associated with higher neuroticism, anxiety, and depression.[78]

In other words, if we don't have a sense of meaning or purpose in our lives, and we start to feel guilty that we don't, and feel pressured to seek it, we can start to get anxious about not having such meaning or purpose.

That is a pretty tough and totally unnecessary way to feel.

Does that mean we ought to give up on having a purpose or meaning in life if we don't already have it?

Of course not. However, what I am suggesting here is another path to discovering your purpose, other than searching for it.

This is where a clarity of intention can help.

In chapter four I outlined the process of defining your various life roles and writing out Applied Positive Intention Statements for the people you impact through those life roles … identifying what you want for someone, and not what you want from them.

Because our relationships are one of the main sources from which we can gain a sense of meaning and purpose, the process of focusing on what we want for other people is like a key that opens the door to gaining a sense of meaning and purpose without having to search for it.

For that reason, if you have not already started, I encourage you to get to work on your Applied Positive Intention Statements for the important relationships in your life.

So, the first step in the Intentional Steps to Trust process is intention and having clear intentions can help us take the second step, and to become more intentional about the promises we make to others and to ourselves.

Promises – the second step in the Intentional Steps to Trust

Once you are clear on your intentions, they guide you to what you can and what you can't promise other people.

You know the old saying, *'Promise what you can deliver and deliver on your promises'*. This old advice is just as important today as it has ever been.

However, it is just as important to know and articulate what you cannot promise; otherwise, the other person could make the mistake of assuming you have promised something.

This is all about being able to set and manage the expectations of everyone involved. Without a clarity of what can and cannot be promised, expectations can be based on assumptions and not on reality.

If, for example, you went to seek advice from a financial planner, unless the planner makes it clear that they *cannot promise* investments in the stock market will always achieve a positive return, you might assume that they can – after all, isn't that what every investor wants … a positive return on their investments?

However, the share market will have good days and not so good days, and some downright disastrous days (and longer).

Trust between a financial adviser and their client is on shaky ground if the risks that are involved in investing in the stock market have not been fully disclosed.

There are other words we can use in place of the word 'promise' when we communicate with others. For example, commitments or assurances, but they still are interpreted by the other person very quickly as something you have promised.

Here's an example where Liz and I were looking to find a builder to do a back-porch extension to our home.

Background: We had received a quote for the project via email from Pete (the builder) on a Friday. I sent Pete a reply email with a couple of questions on the following Monday.

I did not hear from Pete that week, so on the Friday I called and left a message on his phone to say I'd sent an email with some questions and could he get back to me.

Pete quickly called me, and we had a short chat and he said he would take a look at the email over the weekend and get back to me on Monday.

This is a series of text messages that we had with the builder. As you read through them, try to pick the words that we interpreted as 'promise' and how often the promises just weren't lived up to.

> *Pete: Hi Dave, I know I said on the phone last week that I'd reply to your email by yesterday, but my apologies for not replying. I'm working through a heap of emails today and I will be up to speed this week and call you on Friday if that's ok. Thanks.*

> *Me: Hi Pete, we are keen to get your response to our questions and comments on the email, and understand you're busy, so look forward to hearing from you Friday.*

Monday the following week ...

Pete: Hi Dave, sorry for not getting back to you on Friday, we are in a final crazy 2 weeks of completing a big job and will definitely get to your email by Tuesday.

Me: Thanks Pete – we are keen to hear your answers to our questions and comments on the email.

Wednesday that week ...

Pete: Hi Dave, I know I was to get back to your email yesterday, but can I pop around on Thursday around 4pm and we can go through it?

Me: Sure Pete, Thursday 4pm works for me – see you then.

Thursday 5.30pm ...

Pete: Hi Dave, I'm just leaving Woollahra so may be a little late. Apologies for late notice.

Me: OK Pete, see you when you get here.

So, we met at 6.15 that evening and went over the quote and made some adjustments to the plan and scope of the work. Pete left, saying he would get the revised quote to me on the following Monday.

Tuesday after the weekend ...

Me: Hey Pete, just wondering how you're progressing with the porch extension quote?

Pete: Pretty close, just got the final part to finish up tonight. I'll definitely be sending it tomorrow during the day at the latest. Got your email also about the timber cladding – I've used it before it will look great.

Me: Thanks Pete – and glad you agree with the cladding. I look forward to receiving revised quote.

Thursday the following week …

> *Me: Hey Pete how are you going with the quote? Sorry to pester you but we are keen to see the revisions.*
>
> *Pete: Hi Dave. I've finished updating the quotes. Sorry we had a few last-minute work emergencies to attend to last week. I'm on site pouring concrete today and will email everything to you guys when I'm home later. I can drop by tomorrow afternoon to chat about anything if you need.*
>
> *Me: All good – realized something must be up – I look forward to the email. Cheers.*

The following Tuesday …

> *Me: Hey Pete got your email – thanks … there was no attachment though.*
>
> *Pete: Hi Dave. Sorry I meant to attach it. I've got my laptop with me today so will check and send to you ASAP.*

Friday that week …

> *Me: Hi Pete, haven't received the attachment for the revised quote. I rang today and left a message and sent an email through as well. I'd rather have had the chance to say this to you personally, but we've decided to go with another builder. All the best.*
>
> *Pete: Oh … ok. That's disappointing.*

End of communication with Pete!

I wonder how many versions of *'I promise'* you picked up? The easy answer is way too many!

Now, you may judge me harshly and feel sorry for the builder, but I am a very trusting person. However, I hold people accountable for my trust (we will delve into the risk of trusting others in chapter eight). Pete let me down too many times – he consistently showed how inconsistent he was with keeping promises. Being consistent in the way we demonstrate and live up to our character and competence is one of the core elements of trustworthiness that we cover in chapter nine.

The point I'm trying to make here is that it can be so easy for us in our everyday communication, in business and in our personal lives, to unintentionally make promises or commitments that we either can't or don't live up to.

Once we are clear on our intentions for others … what we want for them and not just what we want from them, it helps for us to become more intentionally and mindfully clear about what we can and what we can't promise.

Actions – the third step in the Intentional Steps to Trust

This then leads us naturally to determining more intentionally, mindfully, and more clearly, what actions we will need to do to 'live up to' our promises and to deliver on our intentions for others.

You've no doubt heard the old saying, *'Actions speak louder than words'*. This is a variation of Aristotle's quote I have been using: "Our actions and behaviours are our morals shown in conduct".

I'm hoping you can see now why the Intentional Steps to Trust is a process – each step leads naturally to helping you achieve the next step.

When you ask yourself, what is your intention for another person or group of people, you are becoming more mindful about what you want for them. You are thinking deeply about *why* you are going to do *what* you are going to do and the *impact* it will have on others.

Importantly, you are applying the Light of Day Test *before* you take any action.

Intentional action means holding yourself accountable to answering this question: *'With this decision I'm about to make or this action I'm about to take, would I make this decision or take this action if it were held up in the light of day for all to see?'*

Each of these steps in the Intentional Steps to Trust process is your guide to living in the light of day – striving to be the best version of you and to finding more immediate and practical meaning and purpose in your life through intentionally making life better for others in some way.

Results – The fourth step in the Intentional Steps to Trust

In addition to a sense of meaning in our lives, another core element that evidence-based research shows to positively impact our overall sense of flourishing and wellbeing in our professional and personal lives is to have a sense of achievement.[79]

This is experienced through the altruistic approach you are practising when following the steps in the Intentional Steps to Trust process.

As highlighted earlier, we draw an immense sense of meaning, purpose, and wellbeing when we achieve positive results for others. This is the positive paradox of altruism.

When we do good for others and intentionally make life better for them in some way, it is good for us too … we gain a sense of meaning, purpose, and achievement. All of which helps add to our sense of flourishing and wellbeing.

What's key here is that the Intentional Steps to Trust will more likely (but not always) lead to intentional results that make life better for others – because you start with intention – a mindful awareness of why you are going to do what you are going to do and the impact it will have on others.

It is important to come to terms with the reality that not everything will always lead to the results we intended.

Stuff gets in the way sometimes ... other people can let us down, we can let ourselves down, and other unexpected or unplanned-for disruptive stuff can just get in the way and upset our intended plans.

This is what George Bernard Shaw means in his famous quote of "Life wasn't meant to be easy my child but take courage: it can be delightful".

So, life is not meant to always be easy, but with courage and intention it can be pretty special most of the time.

I think an even better piece of advice to reflect on when stuff just goes wrong in our lives and we don't achieve the results we intended, can be taken from M. Scott Peck's classic book, *The Road Less Travelled.*

He begins with "Life is difficult".

But this is where Peck's next piece of advice is so liberating where he writes: "Once we truly know that life is difficult – once we truly understand and accept it – then life is no longer difficult. Because once it is accepted, the fact that life is difficult no longer matters".[80]

This is what I refer to as an inescapable truth – once we realise and accept that life isn't easy ... it gets easier.

The not-so-easy part of that, of course, is 'accepting' that life is not easy.

Because life isn't easy, we experience many 'little' examples of how our intentional actions, based on our intentional promises, just don't achieve our intentional results.

For example, Liz and I live in Sydney. The traffic in Sydney is like a moving carpark at times. I've come to terms with this and try and allow more than enough time to drive to appointments with clients when I can't catch public transport – which quite often in Sydney can also be difficult (especially with the social distancing required of us during the Covid-19 pandemic).

However, even when I allow what I think is more than enough time to get to an appointment, I also realise that accidents can happen and this can throw my chances of arriving on time out the car window (so to speak).

Here's the thing ... if you're going to be late, make a simple call to the client to let them know, and most reasonable people (also having to deal with the same traffic issues) will accept and, where possible, be flexible enough to shift things around – or we reschedule.

The reality is that life is not easy. Sydney traffic is not easy. I accept it, and when it just lives up to my expectations of being a disastrous morning commute, I can quite easily remain calm, relaxed, make the call to the client, and chill and listen to music or a podcast. Or just take in the entertainment of the many red-faced drivers who are hitting their steering wheels and shouting and beeping their horns – the ones who have not realised and accepted that life isn't easy.

Now, I'm not for one minute saying that I am calm at all times – sometimes it's so easy to forget that life isn't easy ... that this shouldn't be happening and that I don't want it to be this way ... and, like so many others, I just 'lose it'.

But with practice (mostly), it doesn't take me long to realise 'losing it' doesn't make it better – sure it lets off some emotional steam (and I'm ready to admit that can feel pretty darn good), but it doesn't change things ... and so I can (mostly) relatively quickly realise it's easier to accept, be present, and do whatever I can to make the best of an uneasy situation.

What I hope you can take from this discussion on the Intentional Steps to Trust is that it's a process and guide to living in the light of day – of being more intentional about your choices and actions, and when you are you're more likely to achieve intentional results.

Even when your intentional results aren't achieved because of some stuff that just gets in the way, at least you know that the negative outcome was not intentional.

This is important, and it leads to why trust is the final step in the Intentional Steps to Trust process.

Trust – the final step in the Intentional Steps to Trust

When your intentional results have in some way improved the life of others in your professional and personal relationships, you've earned their trust.

However, when the results of your actions negatively impact other people, and those results were not intentional, you can still take the final step in the Intentional Steps to Trust and earn trust, because the other person realises it was always your intention to positively impact their life, despite this negative outcome.

The key here, of course, which we will explore further throughout this book, is what you do next to maintain your trustworthiness.

You see, when you unintentionally make a mistake, and it is clear it wasn't your intention to do so, you haven't breached trust – you're still trustworthy, you just made a mistake.

In these situations it is not about rebuilding trust – it is reconfirming your trustworthiness through your genuine apology, a restatement of your intentions to make life better for the other person, to be clear about what you can and can't promise, to be transparent in what you're going to do to remedy the situation, and to keep the other person updated on your progress.

This is different from earlier examples I have provided of intentional professional and personal breaches of trust. These were not unintentional mistakes; they were intentional choices and acts of deception.

The first step in the Intentional Steps to Trust is intention, and to be living in the light of day that means Applied Positive Intentions – not applied negative intentions.

Let's summarise

To define trust is difficult because we all look at what it means through different lenses and experiences.

One way to define trust, however, is to say it is a firm belief in the reliability, truth and ability of someone or something to deliver an expected result or outcome.

I've shown how trust impacts almost every moment of our lives and provided you with a process for the Intentional Steps to Trust to help guide you to be living in the light of day, striving to be the best version of you, so that you can live an even more meaningful, flourishing, and prosperous life.

While this might all seem very involved, the reality is: get the foundations right and Living in the Light of Day through earning, building, and maintaining more trust in your life becomes a natural part of everyday life.
Those foundations are:

1. Start with a clear and positive intention to make life better for others by being mindfully aware of *why* you are going to do what you're going to do and the *impact* it will have on others.

2. Check in on your choices and actions before you make them by applying the Light of Day Test and continually asking yourself: *Would I make this decision or take this action if it were held up in the light of day for all to see?*

In the next chapter we continue to broaden our understanding of trust, and I will introduce you to three lenses through which you can look at trust in your life: The lens of ***self-trust***, the lens of ***trust others***, and the lens of ***earning others' trust***.

Chapter Five Summary

Trust is a firm belief in the truth, ability or reliability of someone or something to deliver an expected result or outcome. People WILL get your truth. Over time, your intentions, promises, actions and results will either promote you as trustworthy or expose you as not.

"Trust is fundamental to almost every action, relationship and transaction."

Rachel Botsman

Chapter Six

Three lenses of trust

Living in the light of day means holding ourselves accountable for being more intentional in our lives.

To do this means being more proactively and mindfully aware of *why* we intend to do *what* we intend to do and being clear about the *impact* of that intended decision or action on others and not just on ourselves.

As we get clear on our positive intentions to make life better for others, we can better set and manage the expectations of others on what we can and what we cannot promise them.

Being more intentional about this helps us to gain clarity about what we need to do to deliver on the promises we have made to others (and to ourselves).

When we act more intentionally this altruistic approach to life boosts our own sense of wellbeing and helps us to flourish in our professional and personal lives.

Being more intentional is central to living in the light of day and to helping us develop more positive, nurturing, supportive, and trust-based relationships in our lives.

This again helps us to boost our sense of wellbeing and to flourish, both professionally and personally.

In the previous chapters we have considered what it means to trust, and defined trust as *a firm belief in the reliability, truth or ability of someone or something to deliver an expected result or outcome.*

In this chapter we are going to consider what it means to trust through three lenses that have been built into the model below that I refer to as the Triangle of Three Trusts.

As you can see in the model, at the bottom and pointy end of the inverted triangle is the lens of self-trust.

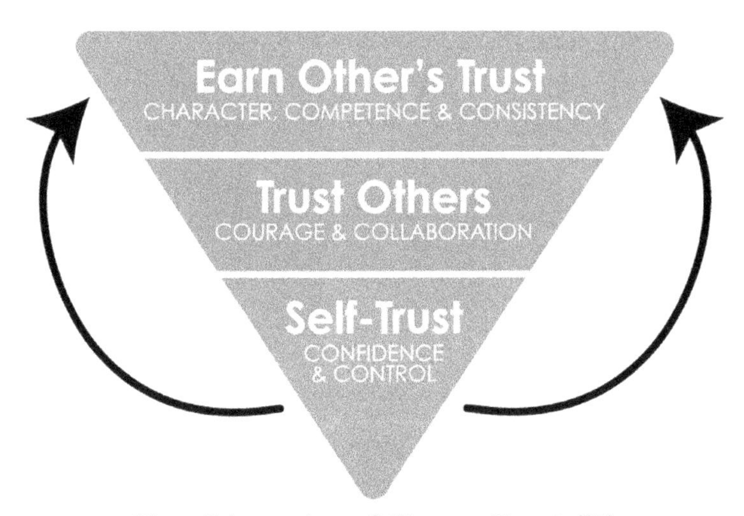

The Triangle of Three Trusts™

Self-trust

I have purposefully inverted the triangle in this model to give the visual effect of the importance of getting self-trust right.

If we do not have a well-balanced sense of self-trust then it is going to be difficult to trust others, and certainly difficult to earn others' trust.

As you look at the inverted triangle, try to imagine it slightly wavering from side to side, as if your self-trust were a bit like a circus acrobat who was balancing a couple of other people on his or her shoulders.

The more balanced, stable, and stronger your self-trust, the more you will be able to balance the amount of trust you place in others, and the more you will be able to earn others' trust.

You can see in the model that self-trust is (among other things) a combination of confidence and control.

The confidence component of self-trust is confidence in your sense that you are a person of good character, that you're competent to achieve in your professional and personal life, and that you are consistent in applying your good character and competence across your life roles.

You'll notice that these three elements (character, competence, and consistency) are the same as those required for you to earn others' trust (the top lens of trust in our Triangle of Three Trusts).

The control component of self-trust is referring to your capacity, motivation, willpower, and discipline to consistently and intentionally make choices and decisions, and to take actions that are aligned with your personal values. It helps you to be living in the light of day, striving to be authentic and the best version of yourself that you can be, and to live a meaningful, flourishing, and prosperous personal and professional life.

In my conference keynote presentations and masterclasses, I ask audience members this question: "How many of you, by raising your hand, would say that you trust yourself?" Almost everyone in the audience will quickly raise their hands.

I then will ask, "And now, being honest with yourself and with the other audience members, how many of you can honestly say that there have been a few times in your life where you might have let yourself down … maybe by having that extra glass (or bottle) of wine, or not exercising, or not having that important conversation when you needed to, or eating a little more chocolate – or that whole block of chocolate?"

Again, and often with a few nervous giggles, almost all of the audience will raise their hands – although also often, the hands are raised more tentatively as the audience members check on how many others around them are prepared to admit that at times they might not have lived up to their own self-trust.

When I first started as a Learning and Development Specialist for a state-based bank in Australia, my manager and the person who hired me was Allan Reidy.

Allan was one of those very rare leaders who believed leadership was a privilege and not just a position. He had this amazing gift of seeing more in his people than they typically saw in themselves.

That was certainly the case with me.

I remember going to Allan soon after I started working with him and saying that I had some self-doubt about my capacity to do the job that I was being asked to do. Allan responded by saying, "David, we hired you for what you can do, for who you are and for all that we believe you will be able to do and who you can become. Anything you can't do or are not confident in, we can work together on a development plan to fix it".

What a gift that was.

In our world, especially in the fast-paced and always-switched-on noise that shouts at us from various social media platforms, it's so easy to start comparing ourselves to others who seem to have more, know more, do more and do better than us, that we can start to lose or at the very least question our self-trust … especially the confidence component of self-trust.

That is not to say we ought to be aiming for perfection.

Indeed, as Brené Brown points out in her wonderfully written book, *The Gifts of Imperfection*,[81] "Perfectionism is the belief that if we live perfect, look perfect, and act perfect, we can minimize or avoid the pain of blame, judgment and shame." Brown also explains that healthy striving is self-focused and asks the question 'How can I improve?' Whereas perfectionism is other-focused and asks the question 'What will they think of me?'

Our self-trust is at risk when we start questioning our own character and competence or our capacity to consistently apply them to the best of our ability in our everyday life.

The confidence component of self-trust is not about being perfect, nor is it about it being so far up yourself that you have not seen daylight for years.

Ok … that was a bit crass, but you know what I mean, don't you. Some people have so much confidence in themselves that it goes beyond a sense of self-trust to a sense of overconfidence and superiority.

Interestingly, research shows that more often than not these overconfident types are found to be shielding a sense of self-doubt and fear underperforming compared to other people.[82]

If you think about your own sense of self-trust you will probably agree that while you might trust yourself in certain situations, in others you might not trust yourself as much.

For example, if you are a naturally disciplined student, you might trust yourself to take on a course of study by distance learning, where you do not need to attend classes. Whereas, if you are the type of student who thrives on working with others and the requirement of turning up to classes, then you might not trust yourself to take on a distance learning course.

In the next chapter we will explore this lens of self-trust in more depth and we will consider other 'self' concepts, including self-worth, self-efficacy, and self-esteem. While these concepts have some similarities, they are different and distinct from each other, and they all impact or are impacted by self-trust. I will also provide you with some evidence-based strategies to help you develop and nurture your self-trust.

Referring back to our Triangle of Three Trusts, resting on self-trust is the lens of trust others.

Trust others

You can see in the model that 'trust others' is (among other things) a combination of courage and collaboration.

The 'courage' component points to the fact that whenever you place your trust in others you're taking a risk – a risk that this other person will live up to your expectations, do what you hope they will do, be who you hope they will be, and deliver on any promise or commitment they have given to you.

This takes courage, because if they let you down in some way, more than likely there will be some negative impact on you.

This courage to trust others is especially evident when it comes to our personal relationships.

According to the online dating site *e-Harmony*, 53 per cent of people lie on their online dating profile. The three main areas they lie about are (1) their age, (2) their weight or height, and (3) their job or income.[83]

For those who lie online, there's more than likely an issue of a low sense of self-trust and, of course, when someone has the courage to place their trust in another person, only to discover that their trust has been breached by a lie, their level of courage to place their trust in others is depleted.

Collaborating with others

Beyond our personal relationships, though, to trust others – whether in our personal or professional life – as you can see in the Triangle of Three Trusts, in addition to the component of courage required, there's also the component of collaboration.

Much of our success, both professionally and personally, will depend on how effectively we can collaborate with others to complete tasks, achieve goals, and experience life.

To collaborate quite simply means to work with others. However, this is not always that simple. In chapter eight we will explore the many benefits we can gain when we have the courage to trust others and collaborate with them and also highlight what can go wrong – especially when collaborating in relationships that lack trust, where trust is at risk or where trust has been breached.

For now, though, as we look through this lens of trust others, what we are basically deciding is whether the other person or people have the combined character, competence and consistency (in demonstrating their 'good' character and competence) that we believe they need for us to trust them and to collaborate with them.

Earn others' trust

Let's return for a moment to the definition of trust that I provided in chapter five: *a firm belief in the truth, ability or reliability of someone or something to deliver an expected result or outcome.*

For reasons that will become clearer to you soon, I am now going to exchange the word truth with *character*; we will exchange the word ability with *competence*, and we will exchange the word reliability with *consistency*. To complete our revised definition, we will also replace 'or' with 'and'.

This means our definition of trust is now:

A firm belief in the character, competence and consistency of someone or something to deliver an expected result or outcome.

As you can see in our Triangle of Three Trusts, character, competence and consistency are the basis on which other people will make their assessment of whether we can earn their trust (as shown in the third lens of trust – earn others' trust).

Chapter nine is devoted to this third lens of trust. For now, though, it's worthwhile to highlight that if you are a person of 'good' character, but you lack the competence (skills, knowledge or resources) that I expect you to have, my trust in you will be somewhat in question.

This is how others will assess my trustworthiness as well.

Similarly, if you have all the competence I expect you to have, but I have a question in my mind regarding your character, your morals, your values, your intentions or what I believe to be your motivation, my trust in you will be in question.

Again, this is how others will assess my trustworthiness.

Finally, if I can see that you have the competence and the character for me to place my trust in you, but you aren't consistent in demonstrating them, then again my trust in you will be in question.

And once again, this is how others will assess my trustworthiness too.

So you can see in this discussion that whether we are looking through the lens of self-trust, the lens of trust others or the lens of earn others' trust, the assessment upon which we base our trust is the combined character, competence, and consistency a person has.

In my assessment of whether I have high or low levels of self-trust, I am determining this on whether I believe I have the character, competence, and consistency to trust myself.

In my assessment of whether I will have the courage to collaborate and trust others, I'm determining my trust in others based on whether I believe they have the combined character, competence, and consistency I require for me to trust them.

And finally, other people's assessment of my trustworthiness is based on their perceptions as to whether I have the combined character, competence, and consistency they require of me, to earn their trust.

As part of my ongoing research into trust, I ask audience members to think about these three lenses of trust, and which of them they believe they need to work on most to help them be more successful in their professional and personal lives.

Let me pause here for a moment and ask you that very question … over the next three months, improvement in which of these three lenses of trust do you believe would help you be even more successful in your professional and personal life?

Now that you have taken the time to consider your answer, here's what my research has shown.

Seventy per cent of people are saying that the area of trust they are struggling most with and could improve on, is the lens of trust others. Twenty per cent are saying they need to work on the lens of self-trust, and ten per cent are saying they need to work on their own trustworthiness – the lens of earn others' trust.

If you consider those numbers for a moment, one interpretation is this: only ten per cent of people believe they need to work on their own trustworthiness – said another way, 90 per cent of people believe themselves to be trustworthy, and that they don't really need to do any work on improving that.

However, at the same time, 70 per cent of people are saying their biggest issue is finding the courage to collaborate and trust others.

In my follow-up interviews, what became evident was that people were feeling so time pressured, being asked to do more with less, and with the constant pace of change and disruption in their lives, that they found it easier to just do things themselves rather than bother about finding the courage to collaborate, delegate or trust others to do things for them.

(It will be an interesting piece of research to explore this again and see how or if the Covid-19 pandemic impacts these findings.)

The issue here, especially in the world of work, is that as more people are taking on more and more, without collaborating, delegating or trusting others to help them, they are experiencing an increased sense of overwhelm … and this comes at a high cost.

According to the American Institute of Stress up to 83% of U.S. workers suffer from work-related stress, costing business an estimated $300 billion in lost productivity.[84] The U.K. Health Foundation reports up to 70 million workdays are estimated to be lost annually from mental health issues with workers.[85] And in a 2019 report by Beyond Blue and TNS Social Research group, titled 'State of Workplace Mental Health in Australia',[86] the research shows one in five Australian employees report they have been off work due to feeling mentally unwell in the previous 12 months.

Aside from the negative impact on workers' wellbeing, from a financial perspective, the report shows the overwhelm people are feeling in the workplace – and the associated untreated mental health conditions – cost workplaces billions per year in absenteeism, presenteeism and compensation claims.

This highlights that when there is a lack of trust – through whatever lens of trust we look – or when trust is at risk, it can have a significantly detrimental impact across our professional and personal lives.

So, what to do about this?

Former President of the United States Calvin Coolidge has been quoted as saying, "Those who leave trust to chance, must abide by the results of chance". My way of saying this is, "If you leave trust to chance, chances are you'll just leave it".

It's clear from the research, we can't leave trust to chance, and we can't afford to reactively wait until trust has been breached (ether intentionally or unintentionally). We need to take proactive steps to be living in the light of day – to be building character, to be earning trust, and to be acting with integrity in all we do.

Here's the thing – we cannot trust everyone 100 per cent of the time, but the one person we have more control over than anyone else, the one person we need to start this journey with, is ourselves.

So, let us take a deeper dive into the first lens of trust – the confidence and control required for self-trust'.

Chapter Six Summary

We all get that trust is important, but sometimes we can just take it for granted, and this puts trust in our lives at risk. Use the three lenses of trust to keep trust at top of mind and action in your life. The three lenses of trust are: the confidence and control required for self-trust; the courage and collaboration required to trust others; and the character, competence and consistency required to earn others' trust.

"This above all: to thine own self be true."

William Shakespeare

Chapter Seven

The confidence and control for self-trust

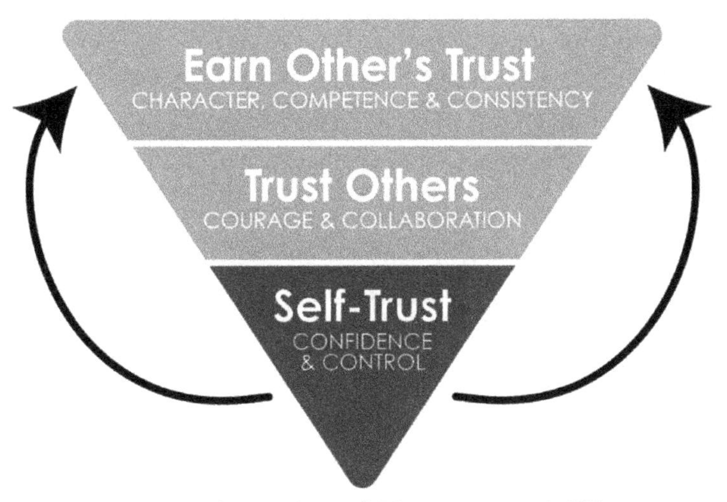

The Triangle of Three Trusts™

Have you ever watched a toddler taking their first steps? Even as I write this, I have got a big smile on my face as I remember that time for each of our two sons.

With our first-born, Matthew, I remember sitting on one of our lounge chairs with Matty standing between my extended legs and using them to hold himself up. He would tentatively walk forward from my thighs out to my ankles and then come back again, continually balancing with his hands on my legs like the rails on a balustrade.

Then the moment came when he got to my ankles and took his first step toward Liz, who was kneeling on the carpet about a metre away, waiting with arms extended and lots of encouragement.

He took his first step, then another, and then fell.

No tears, no disappointment, just a determination to get up by himself, balance and take off again. This time he made it into Liz's arms, and we all carried on as if he had just won the 100-metre sprint at the Olympics. And it was the same with our other son, Anthony.

Toddlers are so determined. They lack fear. They are so keen to learn. Everything seems to be an adventure and a new marvel as they discover more and more about their environment, the people around them, and themselves.

There is a moment in all our lives when we realise that where we were once dependent on others for everything in our life, we ourselves can cause things to happen.

This is what psychologists refer to as *causal agency* – the belief and feelings we have about the control we have over our own actions, and the consequences of those actions.[87]

From infancy we quickly learn that our actions impact ourselves and others, and those actions have consequences. We also learn that sometimes our actions and their impact are intended, and sometimes unintentional.

On my tenth birthday, my best friend Greg and I were double dinking on my brand new Malvern Star Dragster bike. I was on the seat pedalling and Greg was sitting behind me (the Dragster had really long seats, made for two people), when I lost control and we crashed.

Crashing was not an intentional action, and the consequences of the action certainly weren't intended either – I ended up in hospital with concussion (thankfully Greg just received a couple of scratches and bruises).

As we start to do a deep dive into this lens of self-trust, I want to make it very clear that we can't control everything in our lives, and not everything that will happen to us will be intentional.

This reminds me of the German philosopher Reinhold Niebuhr's 'Serenity Prayer' that my mum had on a poster pinned to the inside of the door of our toilet (sorry for that imagery, but it was a prayer that I got to see a lot when I was growing up) ...

"God, grant me the serenity to accept the things I cannot change, the courage to change the things I can, and the wisdom to know the difference."

While it is certainly the reality that you can't control everything in your life, your sense of self-trust will be the driving force behind how you are able to intentionally take appropriate and positive action and respond to whatever life deals you ... and the key words here are *intentionally appropriate and positive action.*

Intentionally appropriate and positive action is what Professor Sonja Lyubomirsky highlights as one of the most significant contributors to our overall sense of wellbeing.[88]

A broad section of researchers in the field of positive psychology, and much of the mainstream self-help world, are using research from Lyubomirsky and her colleague Professor Kennon Sheldon's[89] original suggestion that 50 per cent of our happiness is attributed to our genes, 10 per cent to our circumstances, and 40 per cent to our intentional choices and activities. This has become popularly known as the 'Happiness Pie'.

However, there are several psychology researchers who have criticised Lyubomirsky's and Sheldon's work (for example, Todd Kashdan,[90] Nicholas Brown and Julia Rohrer[91]) for flaws in the research methodology, and noting the reality that our genes, circumstances, choices and actions all impact and interact with each other.

While Sheldon and Lyubomirsky have agreed with some of the criticism, what most if not all positive psychology researchers seem to agree on is this important point – the intentional choices, behaviours, and habits we engage in do matter![92]

What is important from this research, and the key point here, is our capacity to hold ourselves accountable and be more intentional about our choices and actions.

This demonstrates again the importance of getting clear on what our intentions are – how we want to make the world a better place in some way for the people we impact through our professional and personal relationships.

By getting clear on our intentions, we can more clearly communicate what we can and cannot promise others, and this then sets our agenda for the intentional choices and actions we will take to live up to those intentions.

Again, these form the first three steps in our Intentional Steps to Trust model … Step One – intentions, Step Two – promises, Step Three – actions.

We need self-trust to ensure we hold ourselves accountable for living in the light of day … but what is self-trust, how can we develop more of it, and protect ourselves from breaching or losing it?

So, let me ask you at this point the same question I highlighted in the previous chapter: "Do you trust yourself?"

In his book *The Truth About Trust: How it determines success in life, love, learning, and more*, Dr David DeSteno asks this question in a slightly different way: "Are you a fair and honest person?"[93]

It certainly was not a surprise for me, based on my own experiences, that DeSteno's research validates that almost everyone answers yes.

To test whether this is actually true or not, DeSteno and his colleague, Associate Professor Piercarlo Valdesolo from Claremont McKenna College, conducted an experiment where volunteers were placed in a room alone and asked to flip a coin and to record their result. If the result was a head, the participant got to play a 'short, fun video game'. If the result was a tail, the participant got to complete '45 minutes of boring, onerous work'. To make things even more interesting, the participants were told that there was another volunteer in the other room, and that the other volunteer would end up doing whatever was required as a result of the opposite of the coin flip.

What were the findings?

DeSteno reported that 90 per cent of participants either didn't flip the coin (and simply recorded a head, resulting in them getting to play the game), or they kept flipping until they got the 'heads' result they wanted.

As DeSteno writes, "Albeit for different reasons, predicting our own behavior is often no easier than is predicting that of others, even though it certainly feels like it should be".

To discover how we can improve our self-trust and for us to live up to that in reality, we need to understand what we mean when we so readily agree that we are fair, honest, and that we can trust ourselves.

Self-trust is the combination of our confidence (and pride) in our abilities (our competence); our confidence (and pride) in who we are and what we represent to the world (our character); and our sense of control (and discipline) we have in making the intentional choices and actions to consistently demonstrate striving to be the best version of ourselves.

Before we take a look at what the evidence-based research recommends to help us build and protect our sense of self-trust, I want to explore with you a few other 'senses of self' that are often referred to.

Self-Esteem

Let's start with arguably one of the most used terms … self-esteem.

Self-esteem is a combination of your beliefs about yourself and your feelings about those beliefs. When you think about your own self-esteem, you might want to think about how accepting you are of who you are most of the time … what psychologists refer to as self-acceptance. You might also think about your self-esteem in terms of the degree to which you respect yourself – self-respect.

What is important about self-esteem is that it's your own perception or a belief about yourself. A person could have a high sense of self-esteem but could be judged by others as lacking in competence or character.

For this reason, self-esteem is different to self-trust.

You might have a high sense of self-esteem – that you are very accepting of who you are most of the time, and that you have got a high degree of self-respect.

However, in a certain situation you might doubt whether you have the competence to successfully undertake a given task, or you might question whether you have the willpower or discipline to stick at something or resist something. These are examples of a lack of self-trust.

Self-Acceptance

What about self-acceptance?

Again, self-acceptance is different to self-trust.

Self-acceptance is similar to self-esteem but is more of a positive assessment of who you are right now; and as you reflect on your past, it's a positive assessment of who you believe yourself to have been and of what, why and how you went about doing what you've done. Self-acceptance is also an acceptance of your imperfections.

However, that is not an assessment about your competence to successfully undertake a given task; nor is it an assessment as to whether you have the willpower or discipline to stick at something or resist something. Again, these are examples of self-trust and they differ from self-acceptance.

While not widely used in general conversation, one of the most researched senses of 'self' in philosophy, psychology, and social science is self-efficacy.

Self-Efficacy

Self-efficacy refers to the way people think about their competence ... an assessment of their skills and knowledge to effectively get the stuff done in their lives that they want to get done.

In addition, self-efficacy is also a person's belief about how effectively they can and do use their competence in any given situation.

Taking this assessment of oneself a little further, self-efficacy is also a person's belief and feelings about how much 'in control' they are over their own actions and the consequences of those actions. Again, this is what psychologists refer to as 'causal agency'.[94]

But as I said, self-efficacy is not a term that most of us outside of the world of academia use … what we use instead is self-trust.

Self-Trust

When most of us think about what it means to have self-trust, to trust ourselves, what we are typically thinking about is whether we have the skills, knowledge and capacity to achieve what we want to achieve in any given situation. We are also typically thinking about the sense of control we have over our choices and actions … do we trust the choices and decisions we make and the actions we take to achieve what we want to achieve? And finally, we are also mindfully and intentionally considering our sense of control over the consequences of our decisions and actions, not only on ourselves but on others who are impacted by them.

This is why self-trust is essential for us to be living in the light of day.

In fact, world-renowned researcher on self-efficacy, Professor James Maddux of the Center for the Advancement of Well-Being at George Mason University in Fairfax, Virginia, explains it this way: "Most philosophers and psychological theorists agree that a sense of control over our behaviour, our environment and our own thoughts and feelings is essential for happiness and a sense of psychological well-being".[95]

As part of self-trust (or self-efficacy), this 'sense of control' over our environment, our thoughts, feelings, decisions and actions, not only – as Professor Maddux suggests – impacts our happiness and wellbeing; it also directly impacts our levels of motivation.

This 'sense of control' is what I have highlighted earlier in this book that researchers Edward Deci and Richard Ryan refer to as 'autonomy'.

Just to recap for you, in their research Deci and Ryan developed the Self-Determination Theory, which identifies three innate drives for human motivation and flourishing: autonomy, competence, and relatedness.[96]

Autonomy in Self-Determination Theory is not about working in isolation from others. Rather, it is the belief or feeling an individual has regarding their sense of personal control over their choices, decisions, thoughts, feelings, actions, and the consequences of those actions on themselves and on others.

Competence as they refer to it is an individual's belief about their level of skills and abilities in any given situation, and their effectiveness in achieving the desired results in applying those skills and abilities.

Relatedness in Self-Determination Theory is essentially about our sense of feeling socially connected, of belonging and being accepted in nurturing and supportive relationships in our life. Relatedness is the experience we have and feel when we are both cared for and, equally important, when we care for others.

Relatedness also includes the relationship we have with ourselves, which takes us back to our earlier discussion on both self-esteem and self-acceptance.

I mentioned earlier that if you were to ask most people whether they trust themselves, the majority will say yes. Most people will also admit that at times they let themselves down ... and that's only human – we are not perfect, and we will all make unintentional mistakes, and occasionally make poor decisions that are goal distracting rather than goal supportive.

There is a question about self-trust we need to consider here, and I will paraphrase (sloppily I will admit) the great words of Shakespeare – *To self-trust or not to self-trust? That is the question.*

Most if not all of us have weaknesses. Two (of many) of mine are rum and raisin chocolate (I'm not brand dependent) and red wine (maybe a little more selective here) … I just love the stuff. I'm not kidding when I share with you that every now and then I've totally overindulged, and I'm also ready to admit there's a chance that in the future I might occasionally overindulge again. (Judge me as you will … remember, none of us is perfect.)

Here is the thing, though – it is only occasionally that I overindulge; it's not a habit.

In the Light of Day Test you'll remember whenever we are about to make a decision or take an action, we can ask ourselves, 'Would I make this decision or take this action if they were held up in the light of day for all to see?'

As we are discussing self-trust here, I'd like to now share with you a variation of the Light of Day Test:

Is the decision I am about to make or the action I am about to take moving me toward living by my personal values or moving me away from it?

The original version of the Light of Day Test is asking us to consider our decisions and actions if, before we made the decision or took the action, other people in our lives would approve.

This second version introduces the importance of having personal values that we can use as our guide in choosing decisions and actions that help us strive to live our lives in a way that represents the best version of ourselves.

Let me again remind you here of Aristotle's advice when he wrote, "Our actions and our behaviours are our morals shown in conduct". We can replace the word 'morals' with 'values'.

It's not what you think or feel, it's what you do that matters most ... and if what you do is mindfully and intentionally done in alignment with your values, you will be living in the light of day, and making better choices and decisions and doing more positive things to help you strive to be the best version of yourself.

Dr Russ Harris is one of the world's leading authorities on the scientifically proven mindfulness-based approach of Acceptance and Commitment Therapy (ACT). In his book, *The Reality Slap*, Harris explains values in this way:[97]

"[Values] are your heart's deepest desires for how you want to behave as a human being; they are the qualities you want to bring to your ongoing actions. They are different to goals in that goals can be completed or achieved, ticked off the list and finished; whereas values are ongoing until the day you die".

We will explore values in more detail later in this chapter, and I will provide you with some ideas on how to check in on and clarify your values in an easy and practical way.

You see, a person might complete a goal, but the question is, especially as it relates to self-trust, did they achieve the goal in a way that makes them proud ... in a way that represented them as the best version of themselves?

Many years ago, when I was working with one of Australia's most successful recruitment and consulting companies, I saw many examples of candidates who were trying to achieve the goal of securing a new job or career, only to be thwarted when they were 'found out' to be lying on their application or resumé.

Let me remind you again ... people will get your truth: Over time, your intentions, promises, actions, and results will either promote you as trustworthy or expose you as untrustworthy.

In the 1980s the then head of Scandinavian Airlines, Jan Carlzon, coined the phrase 'moments of truth', referring to the moments when a customer's experience results in a choice as to whether they will buy or not buy a product or service.[98]

Just like these moments of truth – where we as consumers have an experience that brings up either pleasant or not-so-pleasant thoughts and feelings, upon which we choose whether to buy or not buy a product or service – throughout our day we all have moments of truth where we choose to do things that either move us toward a better life or move us away from living a better life.

In another book, *ACT Made Simple,* Dr Russ Harris refers to these moments of truth as a *choice point.*[99]

So, we all have these moments of truth, these choice points throughout our day, and being aware that this is happening is so important when it comes to self-trust.

You see, we need to be able to trust ourselves so that we can mindfully and intentionally choose more actions that move us toward being our best version of ourselves and choose fewer actions that move us away from this goal.

That is not always easy though, is it!

On days when everything is going well for us, choosing to take action that helps us to flourish in life is much easier. But life does not always go to plan … life isn't always easy.

On days when we face some tough stuff that life dishes out from time to time, we get what can be 'uninvited' and difficult thoughts and feelings. They don't make it easy for us to make mindful and intentional choices to take action that will help us to flourish in life.

We all have this inner voice that is constantly chattering away inside our minds. It's a pretty amazing thing when you think about this inner voice that we all have.

For our son Matthew, that was certainly the case when he first realised that he had an inner voice.

He was about four and half years old and he came running out of his bedroom beaming with excitement, and came up to me and said, "Dad, Dad, guess what I've learned".

I asked, "What is it Matty, what have you learned?"

With that he said, "Watch this. It's really clever" and he stepped a bit closer to me, folded his arms and, without saying anything, he looked up at me, gave me a big knowing smile and just nodded his head.

Now, he did this without speaking for about ten seconds before I gave in and said, "Matty, I don't get it. What are you doing?"

He laughed and unfolded his arms saying, "I knew you wouldn't get it", and he laughed again and ran back to his room.

So, there I was, a 34-year-old father, standing alone, wondering what had just happened.

But then he came back out from his room. This time he had one of his early reader books with him (he was just starting to learn how to read). With a big smile, he said, "Dad, watch and I will show you what I've learned".

He started to read out loud, slowly following each word on the page with his finger. "John and Jill run", he read and then looked up at me, smiled and then looked back down at the words. "John and Jill jump", he said and again looked up at me, smiled, returned to the book, and turned the page.

This time he didn't read anything out loud, although I could see him looking at each of the words in the next sentence.

He continued to look up at me and back down to the book again until I finally gave in and asked what it was that he had learned that had captured his excitement.

"I knew you wouldn't get it Dad", he said again. "At first I was reading the words from the book out of my mouth, then I stopped and just looked at the words, but I could still hear my voice saying each word inside my head." He looked at me with amazed and excited eyes and asked me, "Can you do that Dad?"

I smiled and said, "Yes Matty, I can. In fact, we all can read silently to ourselves. And that's a really clever thing you've learned".

"Yes, yes Dad, but that's not what I've learned." His ability to keep people's attention has always been an amazing strength and this was an early example of it.

"Then what is it Matty?" I asked again. "What is it that you've learned?"

"Dad, I don't even have to look at the words of a book. I can just say things in my head without reading. But you can't hear them, can you?"

I smiled right back at him and said, "That's right, Matty. I can't hear what you say inside your head".

"I know, I know … that's what I've learned", he said. Matty then took a step forward, looked at me again, crossed his arms and said nothing. He gave me that same knowing smile and it was obvious he was saying something to himself. To this day he still gives me that same look often and, of course, I still don't know what he's saying to himself. (I'm probably better off not knowing most of the time.)

So, that was a very special time when Matty realised he had an inner voice, but at that stage he had only realised his inner voice when he was trying to say things to himself.

He was yet to learn that sometimes our inner voice talks to us in ways that aren't all that pleasant.

Sometimes the reality is that we have positive thoughts and feelings that are welcome, but at other times we have more difficult and challenging thoughts and feelings that we would rather not have.

This is true for all of us – even those overly positive people and motivational speakers ... they too have these tough moments of truth when difficult thoughts and feelings arrive, despite their best efforts to stay positive ... they're often just not prepared to admit it.

That might come as a surprise to you ... it certainly did surprise me when I first realised that all of us – yes, all of us from time to time – find ourselves with difficult thoughts and feelings.

This next point is crucial when it comes to understanding how you can strengthen your self-trust ... While all of us have these difficult thoughts and feelings, we can choose to act in ways that are aligned with our values – regardless of what we are thinking and regardless of what we are feeling.

There are a lot of self-help-positive-thinking-motivational gurus who preach about the power of positive thinking, which is fine, but they often also encourage and advise us to eradicate negative thoughts and feelings, battle with them, and with willpower turn them from negative to positive affirmations.

Should we believe them? That is what researchers Joanne Wood and her colleagues decided to test.

Two experiments they undertook showed that among participants with low self-esteem, those who repeated a positive self-statement, "I'm a lovable person", felt worse than those who did not repeat the statement.

Interestingly, among participants with high self-esteem, those who repeated the statement or focused on how it was true, felt better than those who did not, but only to a limited degree.

Their findings show that repeating positive self-statements may benefit certain people but can backfire for the very people who 'need' them the most.[100]

So, for some people the evidence-based research suggests doing battle with these difficult thoughts and feelings can just amplify them and make it even more difficult to choose to take action that moves you toward being the best version of yourself and living a more flourishing, meaningful, and prosperous life.

One of the most powerful books I've read on this is Professor Steven Hayes' *A Liberated Mind: How to pivot towards what matters.*[101] Professor Hayes is the originator of Acceptance and Commitment Therapy (ACT) that I mentioned earlier.

Hayes' research is extensive, and he has written over 45 books and more than 625 scientific articles. In *A Liberated Mind* he explains how our human minds have developed since we were huddled together in caves, to be constantly on the lookout for danger – just to survive.

You might recall that I mentioned this in chapter two.

As cave dwellers, danger was everywhere. Thinking positively or just being optimistic about life was not going to cut it when around the corner, or behind the next rock, there was a high likelihood of some flesh-eating animal ready to pounce.

So, as humans our minds evolved with this default way of constantly warning us, and whether the danger was real or not, we were constantly taking action to protect ourselves.

Leaping forward to the present day, that part of our cave-dwelling mind remains. We are hard-wired to naturally have thoughts and feelings that are warning us or challenging us about things that may or may not be real.

The problem is, these difficult thoughts and feelings that turn up from time to time aren't very pleasant … and the reactive choices we can typically take when we have these thoughts and feelings are to try and ignore them; try and do battle with them through willpower and affirmations; or give in to them and do things that lessen the volume of the thoughts or numb the feelings in some way to feel better.

We all get pretty good at coming up with these reactions, including doing something more pleasurable that takes our minds off what we're thinking or feeling – eating the whole block of rum and raisin chocolate (oh no … damn you chocolate), or substance abuse (did I mention red wine?).

You are not your thoughts or your feelings

I would like you to try an experiment here. It's an activity that can help you more vividly and consciously notice your thoughts and feelings and help you to realise ways to not get sucked into them, which can hook you into making choices and taking actions that will not be as good for you in the long run.

Just a heads-up here … if you are a cynical type, or someone who is not that 'in touch' with their feelings and emotions, what you're about to read may be quite challenging.

And that's ok.

Just know, this is not self-help rubbish … this is a scientific, evidence-based research approach to help you strive to be the best version of yourself – especially when you are faced with tough times in your life and when you have difficult thoughts and feelings.

It may take courage for you to complete this activity, but please know that it will be worth the effort.

So, this is an exercise to help you see how you are not your thoughts and you are not your feelings, and that you can choose to take appropriate and positive action, regardless of what you think or feel.

With that in mind, I invite you now to read through this section in its entirety first, then do the activity once you have finished reading.

You might find it easier to complete this activity by listening to an MP3 audio I have recorded to guide you through it – you'll find the link to listen online or download it at **https://davidpenglase.com/guided-noticing-audio**

> Take a moment to sit in a chair or on your sofa … sitting forward a little with your back straight and your feet firmly on the ground. If you like you can close your eyes, or just pick a spot on the wall in front of you, or an object directly in your line of sight.
>
> Now take a moment to just notice your breath. You don't need to change your breathing, just notice breathing in and breathing out. Notice as you're breathing in that you might sense your breath is a little cooler and a little warmer as you breathe out. Just do this for a moment … noticing your breath … breathing in and breathing out. As you're breathing in notice where your breath is going … notice the rise and fall of your belly … breathing in … breathing out … notice the rise and fall of your chest … notice the slight movement of your shoulders … keep following your breath … breathing in and breathing out.
>
> Now as you keep breathing normally, notice your feet resting on the ground … you might like to wriggle your toes a little … notice how that feels … keep breathing

normally as you do … now notice your calves … breathing in … breathing out … and now notice your buttocks … notice them pressing against the chair you're sitting on … just stay there noticing them pressing against the chair for a moment more … breathing in … breathing out … now returning to noticing your breathing … in and out … the rise and fall of your stomach … the rise and fall of your chest … the slight movement of your shoulders.

Now notice that there you are, sitting on the chair, breathing in and out … notice any sounds you might be hearing … notice any thoughts you might be thinking … keep breathing normally … breathing in … breathing out … now notice that there's you in the chair, noticing your breathing, noticing the sounds you're hearing, noticing the thoughts that you're thinking … notice that you're noticing all of these things … you're noticing your breathing, you're noticing you sitting in the chair, you're noticing the sounds you're hearing and you're noticing the thoughts that you're thinking.

So, there's you in the chair, there's the sounds you're hearing and the thoughts you're thinking … and there's a noticing part of you noticing all of these things.

Now … as you finish this activity, when you're ready, open your eyes if you've had them closed, gently stretch and maybe stand up and gently stretch a little more … and you've now completed this activity.

Time to do the activity

Ok… now that you have read through the activity, read through it again … and go ahead and complete it. (I realise you can't close your eyes as you're reading ... that's why I've recorded the audio for you.)

As you consider this activity, you might notice yourself thinking of reasons why not to do it. However, you can still choose to do it ... I really do encourage you to, because it's helped me to realise one of the most important lessons I've ever learned: that despite having difficult thoughts and feelings, we don't have to get sucked into them – we can notice them, accept them (even though we may not 'like' or want them) and still take intentional appropriate and positive action anyway.

Now that you've completed the activity (have you?), I'm wondering what you think about it ... I wonder how you feel about it.

Maybe take a moment to jot down your thoughts about what you think and feel about that exercise – and if you're not sure, that's ok too.

This is an activity I recommend you try at least once a day for the next week or so – you might want to even add it as a daily routine – and it's ok if you choose not to.

Here's the realisation that has been one of the most important lessons I've learned in my 60 plus years on this earth ... This noticing part of you isn't your thoughts – because it's *noticing* your thoughts. It isn't your feelings either – because it's *noticing* your feelings.

So, there's your thoughts and feelings, and then you've got this special, separate noticing part of you. This part of you can help you be aware of what you're thinking and feeling. Most importantly, it can help you choose to take action in any situation, regardless of what you think or how you feel.

This vital reality is that your thoughts are just thoughts and your feelings are just feelings, and regardless of what you think or how you feel, no matter how difficult or challenging those thoughts or feelings are, you can choose to not get hooked into them. You can choose to take positive action that is aligned with your personal values to help you strive to be the best version of yourself

– to be living in the light of day. You can choose positive actions – regardless of how your thoughts and feelings might be trying to suck you into worrying about that sabre-toothed tiger hidden behind the next rock.

You don't have to do battle with your thoughts and feelings ... you don't have to try and ignore them (because they may or may not just keep coming back) ... you don't have to try and get rid of them ... they're just thoughts and feelings. The reality is that, regardless of these thoughts and feelings, you can choose to take effective, positive and values-based action.

What I've provided you with here is an introduction to ACT (Acceptance and Commitment Therapy). There is a lot of science, psychology and research on this topic – far too much for me to share with you in this book; however, I have introduced you to two of the world's leading experts on ACT (Steven Hayes – www.stevenhayes.com and Russ Harris – www.actmindfully.com) and I highly recommend you visit their sites and access their resources. They will guide you on learning even more skills and strategies to help you build and maintain this all-important area of self-trust.

Your Personal Values

I've mentioned that one of the most important elements of self-trust is a clarity of your personal values.

If you're not clear on your values, the choice you make – in those moments of truth when life dishes you some tough stuff – could get you sucked into difficult thoughts and feelings and distract you from living in the light of day. It might stop you from choosing actions reflecting the best version of yourself and make it more difficult for you to live a more flourishing, meaningful, and prosperous life.

You might already be very clear on your personal values, but just in case, there are a number of ways, tools and resources available to help you determine the values upon which you would like to live your life and guide you to demonstrate in action the best version of yourself.

You could, for example, jump on Russ Harris' website – www.actmindfully.com.au. Harris has a free resources section and one of the resources is a list of 38 core values.

The World Values Day website (www.worldvaluesday.com/tools-and-resources) has a range of free resources, as well as links to some commercial resources you might want to explore.

Personally, I've been working on my values since my early twenties, when Lew Davies, who was my team leader at the time in the State Bank's training and development division, gave me a book written by Dr Maxwell Maltz – *Psycho-Cybernetics.*[102]

It was that book that I still attribute to this day as being the spark that ignited my academic and experiential fascination with what causes people to think, feel and act the way they do.

While there is much in Maltz's book that now is somewhat outdated, as science and psychology have moved on, the first chapter sparked my interest, and was totally dedicated to the exploration of the self-image.

In that first chapter, Maltz quotes from an article in the magazine *Cosmopolitan* (I know … hardly an evidence-based psychology journal), written by T. F. James, summarising the results obtained by various psychologists and medical doctors: "Understanding the psychology of the self can mean the difference between success and failure, love and hate, bitterness or happiness".

As a 20-year-old I'd never considered this idea of a self-image and the importance of understanding the values upon which we live our life.

So, my journey of self-discovery and academic research over many years started from that book, and part of that journey has been to continually work on determining, reviewing, and refining my core values.

Our personal beliefs over our life span can change as we experience and learn more, but what about our personal values – do they change over our life span?

That's a question Valdiney Gouveia, Professor of Social Psychology at Federal University of Paraíba, Brazil, and his colleagues decided to research.[103]

Drawing from a large sample of over 36,000 participants, ranging in age from 12 to 65, with an even split of male and female, using an instrument called the Basic Values Survey, participants rated the importance of 18 values that were clustered into six core values as follows:

- **Excitement – represented by the values of emotion, pleasure, and sexuality**
- **Promotion – represented by the values of power, prestige, and success**
- **Interaction – represented by the values of affection, belonging, and support**
- **Normative – represented by the values of obedience, religiosity, and tradition**
- **Actualization – represented by the values of beauty, knowledge, and maturity**
- **Existence – represented by the values of health, stability, and survival.**

You might want to do something similar for yourself ... make a list of the 18 values, rating them in their importance to you in your different life roles. Then I'd recommend you look at the values that you've rated most highly and are repetitive across your different life roles. The result should help you to isolate five or six core values from the 18. (I'd personally ignore using the clustered six core values. In my opinion they're a bit too academic in their language and not that practical on a day-to-day basis.)

What the researchers discovered was evidence that suggests that over our lifespan our values can change, or at the very least become more or less important at certain times in our lives.

Interestingly, over the life span, while there were some slight differences, the values of men and women at certain stages of their lives for the most part were similar.

However, as I reflect on my core values, I feel they have been stable for most of my life, although I might have named them differently, and some might not have been as 'core' as others at certain times of my life.

I've been continually determining and refining my values for many years and have tried many approaches. There isn't one 'best' method and I recommend you try a range of ways to determine, review and refine your values at least annually.

Values clarification activity

Here is what I hope you'll find to be a practical and worthwhile guide to help you establish your values:

1. **List your life roles** – Make a list of the different life roles you have. (If you've completed the earlier activity of writing out an Applied Positive Intention statement,

you will already have your list.) These could include, in no particular order (and not a complete list): husband or wife, father or mother, friend, son or daughter, son-or-daughter-in-law, brother or sister, your job role(s), coach, neighbour.

2. **Values writing** – For each life role, take the time to write out how you want to be, what you want to be doing, and how you would hope others would see you in each of those life roles.

3. **Values listing** - Once you've completed the values writing, go back over what you've written and highlight any word that seems to you to be a personal value (words similar to those in the 18 values listed earlier).

4. **Values identification** - Next extract all the highlighted values and list them on a page and note how many times any one value is repeated over the different life roles. Those that are repeated the most are your core values.

5. **Refine** – The final step is to refine these words describing your core values down to a minimum of four and maximum of six.

To illustrate, here is what I ended up with:

- **Vitality – being present and engaged in what I'm doing, and maintaining my physical and mental health**

- **Contribution – using my strengths, knowledge, and talents in whatever way I can to help make life better for others, both professionally and personally**

- **Authenticity – being prepared to be vulnerable, turning up as my best self while acknowledging and being at peace with my imperfections**

- **Learning – being curious and proactively deepening my knowledge, understanding, and perspectives, while being prepared to consider other points of view and experience**

- **Love – genuinely caring for and about others in my life and remembering to let others care for and about me too.**

I share these with you to demonstrate my own work on myself and not to hold these values up as the ones you or anyone else ought to have.

In most of the work I do, I try to find creative ways to make things easier to understand. It might seem a little cheesy to you, but when I realised that with a bit of shuffling my five core values form the acronym VCALL … which I now refer to as my Values CALL.

As I apply the Light of Day Test (the second version I presented to you earlier), I ask myself this question:

Is this action I'm about to take or this decision I'm about to make moving me toward living my values of vitality, contribution, authenticity, learning and love, or moving me away from living my personal values?

So, when life throws some difficult moments when my thoughts and feelings try to get me hooked and distracted from living in the light of day, this is how I can notice my thoughts and feelings; and even when it's difficult (and it often is) to allow those thoughts and feelings to be with me, I can mindfully notice them, acknowledge to myself that they're with me, accept that they are, and that it's ok.

Even though I may not like what I'm thinking or how I'm feeling emotionally and physically, I can use my VCALL as my guide, take action aligned with my values and move more toward being my best version of myself and living a flourishing, meaningful, and prosperous life.

A reality check here, though ... it doesn't always work!

Those pesky and difficult thoughts and feelings that are ingrained in all of our brains from time to time are warning me about that sabre-toothed tiger just around the corner, or of what happened when I ignored them in the past, and how that didn't end up too well for me.

Whether it's when I'm about to go and present to a thousand people at a corporate conference, or when I've had a friend or family member with a terminal illness, or I get stuck in Sydney's typical traffic jam and it's going to cause me to be late for an appointment or miss the start of a movie, most days of my life, in every one of these situations I've listed, there've been times when I've got hooked and distracted by my thoughts and feelings.

When this occurs, rather than immediately using my VCALL to guide my behaviour, if I get sucked into my thoughts and feelings I can get anxious about the presentation; stay way too long ruminating about my inadequacy to be able to change my friend or family member's terminal illness; or I might shout and get angry in my car in frustration at being stuck in traffic.

Here's the thing, though ... over time I've got better at quickly noticing when my actions aren't aligned with my values and know that in that moment of truth I have the choice of taking more appropriate and values-aligned action. And I know, with practice, this can be true for you too.

So, what I'm not saying is that any of this self-trust stuff is easy ... when life's good it's fairly easy, but when life's tough, sometimes we can let ourselves down.

However, if we can be kind to ourselves and know we are not perfect, and that we will every now and then get sucked in by those pesky thoughts and feelings – remember, you, me and everyone else has these difficult thoughts and feelings from time to time … it's only natural. Knowing that we have the choice to notice them for what they are – thoughts and feelings, not us – we can mindfully choose to take more appropriate, values-driven actions, to pivot away from being distracted, and to move toward living in the light of day and being our best versions of ourselves.

Self-trust and goal achievement

As I've highlighted in this chapter, values are not goals. Goals can be set, pursued, and achieved (or not), whereas values are a part of who you are and are displayed through your words and actions.

The key point here is the power of using your values as a guide to help you achieve goals in your professional and personal life.

Humans are aspirational, goal-seeking beings. Goals are not just important for us to achieve and acquire things in our lives, when the goals we set for ourselves are aligned with our personal values, science validates that these types of goals are a key contributor to our overall life satisfaction and wellbeing.[104]

There are many books and resources to help you with goal achievement, but one of my personal favourites is Dr Adam Fraser's book, *Strive*.[105]

Fraser describes striving in this way:

"Striving equals taking on challenging activities that require us to be brave and evolve in the pursuit of something that is purposeful and important. It is a critical and necessary state that leads to huge levels of fulfilment and transformation." And he adds: "The sad reality is most people are not engaging in it nearly enough".

Rather than me delving into goal achievement in this book, I highly recommend you grab a copy of Adam's book, *Strive.* I'm sure you will enjoy the irreverent, funny, and conversational writing style, and importantly the book is based on over ten years of evidence-based research that will lead you through a practical and proven process for goal achievement.

Ok, there's a lot that I've covered in this chapter on self-trust, and so much more that we could explore, but now we need to move onto the second lens of trust in our Triangle of Three Trusts – the lens of trust others.

Chapter Seven Summary

Looking at life through a lens of Self-trust helps to confirm that it's not what you think or feel that matters. What matters is what you choose to do in those important moments in life. When you can clearly determine and articulate your personal values and take mindful and intentional actions that are aligned with your personal values, you will be living in the light of day, and making better choices and decisions and doing more positive things to help you strive to be the best version of yourself.

"Life shrinks or expands in proportion to one's courage."

Anais Nin

Chapter Eight

The courage and collaboration to trust others

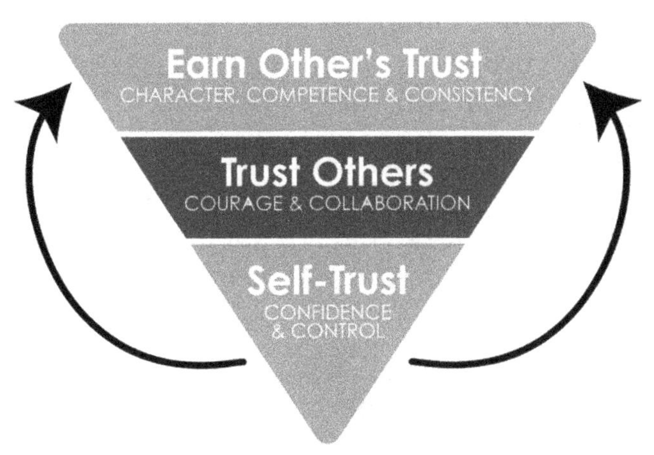

The Triangle of Three Trusts™

Would you say that you are a trusting person – someone who finds it relatively easy and comfortable to trust others?

To trust others is our second lens of trust in the Triangle of Three Trusts, and this is a consideration of what scholars refer to as your *propensity to trust*, which is defined as "an individual's general willingness to trust others".[106]

So, what do you think – do you have a general willingness to place your trust in others and an overall belief that what most people say and do can be trusted?

This is what researchers Detlef Fetchenhauer and David Dunning have been exploring and, in particular, questioning whether we can trust too much or too little.

In one of their experiments they measured the level of scepticism participants had toward trusting a stranger to perform a task that would see both participant and stranger gaining a benefit.[107]

Over three separate experiments participants anticipated that more than 50 per cent of the strangers could not be trusted. However, the results showed their scepticism was unjustified, because almost 80 per cent of the strangers performed the task where both the stranger and the other participant gained mutual benefit.

In a world where the research says many of us are asking ourselves the question, 'Who can we trust?', there is also a large body of research that is telling us our concern and apprehension about trusting others may in the majority of cases be unfounded.

This raises the question, 'What is causing this concern and reluctance to trust others?'

When you were born, your propensity to trust was arguably absolute … you had no real choice other than to trust others. However, as you grew from an infant into childhood, then through your teenage years to whatever age you are now, your propensity to trust has been formed by your life experiences.

Our individual and collective experiences help us to form opinions about who we think we can and cannot trust.

Apparently, most of us think scientists are the most trustworthy professionals and that (perhaps not unsurprisingly) politicians are the most untrustworthy.

This was the finding of a 2019 global survey on which professions are the most trustworthy. The report of the Ipsos Global Trust in Professions survey[108] found the top five most trustworthy professions were:

1. Scientists
2. Doctors
3. Teachers
4. Armed forces
5. Police.

The survey reported the five most untrustworthy professions were:

1. Politicians
2. Government ministers
3. Advertising agencies
4. Bankers
5. Clergy/priests.

The survey also had a category of 'Ordinary men and women', which came in at number 6 globally as trustworthy, just ahead of judges at number 7 and lawyers at number 8.

Now this research only covered certain professions, and there are a lot of other people in various businesses and situations who we might need to trust.

I am wondering how you would rate your propensity to trust your hairdresser, butcher, or the owner-operators of your local fish market or grocery store? What about your propensity to trust salespeople?

When you think about your own inclination to trust others, you might arrive at the conclusion that it all depends on who we are considering placing our trust in, and our experiences with those people.

Sometimes, based on our experiences, we trust others after careful thought and consideration. Psychologists refer to this as 'cognitive trust' ... meaning our trust is based on logical thinking.

Let's consider for a moment some examples of when we might base our trust in others on cognitive trust.

If we have had previous experience with a person or a company, we might simply think deeply about whether they delivered the results we expected and in ways we were happy with.

If we have not had previous experience with a person or a company, we might ask friends, colleagues, or family members what their experiences were. We might research the company's website; we might research online review forums about the company.

If it's a person rather than a company, we might again ask friends, colleagues, or family members about their experiences in dealing with that person. We might do a social media check.

At other times, though, our decision to trust others might not be first based on what we think, but rather purely on how we feel – our emotions tell us to trust with our heart. Psychologists refer to this as 'affective trust' ... meaning our trust is based not on logical thinking, but rather on our gut feeling.[109]

What about you?

Do you think when you place your trust in others your basis for that trust is from your heart (it's something you feel) or from your head (it's something you've thought deeply about)?

To help you consider this a little more deeply, when we 'cognitively-trust' in others, we are more likely to be looking for evidence based on a person's (or company's) reputation, their credibility, what's been reported of their achievements, their consistency in their track record.

When we 'affectively-trust' in others, we are more likely to be basing that trust on a sense that we like the other person (or not) and we will be basing our trust on our gut feeling about not just what the other person is saying, but how they're saying it and what their body language and energy levels are suggesting to us.

The reality is, we will all use both elements of trust (affective–feeling and cognitive–thinking) to determine whether we ought to place our trust in others.

More typically, though – and there is not a lot of empirical research on this – it seems some of us have a preference or more heavy reliance on one or the other.

One thing is certain, however: most of us place a high level of importance on 'word of mouth' testimonials from our friends, colleagues, and family members when it comes to making our decisions to trust others.

However, more and more in our online world, we are turning not just to 'word of mouth' testimonials, but to what is now termed 'word of web', which consists of online testimonials and reviews.

We can now readily search the internet to discover ratings of Uber drivers, an Airbnb owner's property, a café, a restaurant, a holiday destination, or vacation experience.

And of course, as covered earlier in the book, as consumers we too can now be rated by businesses we buy from. For example, Uber drivers can rate us as passengers and Airbnb owners can rate us as guests.

But how reliable are online reviews?

This is a question researchers Dina Mayzlin, Yaniv Dover, and Judith Chevalier have been exploring.[110]

What they were most concerned about were at least two potentially problematic outcomes of fake reviews. The first was that people can be fooled by the promotional reviews and not make the most appropriate choices in their best interest.

The second problem with fake reviews is that they may result in consumers not trusting the very reviews designed to help inform them in their decision to trust or not.

The question that many of us are asking more and more is, of course, how do you detect whether a review or even an online company is fake or real?

The answer, though, is not so easy for most of us to detect, which is why in recent years there has been a rise in online sites like FakeSpot[111] and ReviewMeta[112] that help you check reviews and the legitimacy of online offers.

So, our propensity to trust in both an online and offline world is not only based on our own experiences, or just on what we can learn from 'word of mouth', but also from 'word on web'.

However, what this discussion and the research raises is our propensity or willingness to trust will also be in play when we are deciding whose opinions and experiences, we will use to help us decide on who we can place our trust in.

This is why researchers have been fascinated by our propensity for trust and have developed a range of techniques and experiments to test and assess our comfort and willingness to trust.

The research experiment I introduced earlier in this chapter – between a participant's scepticism toward trusting a stranger to perform a task that would result in mutual gain to both participant and stranger – was one of the most used to measure a range of elements around trust.

It was developed in the field of economics and is known as the *Trust Game.*

In 1995 researcher Joyce Berg and her colleagues[113] decided to test the typically reported economic theory that people will always act in their own self-interest. They developed an experiment where the volunteers were separated into two rooms – room A and room B.

The following are the original instructions given to the volunteers.

- **Each person in room A and each person in room B has been given $10 as a show up fee for this experiment.**
- **Persons in room A will have the opportunity to send in an envelope, some, all, or none of their show up fee to a person in room B.**
- **Each dollar sent to room B will be tripled. For example, if you send an envelope which contains $2, the envelope will contain $6 when it reaches room B. If you send an envelope which contains $9, the envelope will contain $27 when it reaches room B.**
- **The person in room B will then decide how much money to send back to the person in room A and how much money to keep.**

If you were the person in room A, I'm wondering whether you would choose to keep all of your $10, or would you take a risk that the person in room B, on accepting whatever amount you decide to send (and that amount is tripled), would return an amount back to you that would see you financially better off than if you'd simply kept the $10?

What do you think most people would do?

Now, the standard theory of economics at the time was that people will always act in their own self-interest, and the predicted result was that in stage one of the game the person in room A would choose to send nothing and keep their $10. That would mean the person in room B would not receive any money and stage two of the game would not eventuate.

However, in the original experiment by Berg and her colleagues, 30 out of 32 game trials disproved that theory.

What actually happened was in 30 cases the person in room A sent an average of over 50 per cent of their $10. As per the game, this was then tripled by the researcher.

If the theory that people always act in their own self-interest were true, the results of the second stage would be that the person in room B who received the tripled amount of money would keep all of that money and send nothing in return.

However, that also is not what happened.

In fact, on average the person in room B returned an amount that was more than the original (non-tripled) amount sent by the person in room A, and typically they returned in excess of 50 per cent of the tripled amount.

Put simply, both the person in room A and the person in room B increased the amount of money they had because of taking the risk (trusting) that the other person would reciprocate the act of 'giving'.

The Trust Game has been repeated countless times (including the earlier example I provided by Fetchenhauer and Dunning) over many years, and the results of the very first experiment remain consistent.

But you and I both know games are not necessarily real life – other elements and contexts are involved in real life that are not involved in a game.

Perhaps as you think about this, you might come to the conclusion that your propensity to trust in others is like so many other things in our lives: that it 'all depends' … it all depends on this other person you are considering to trust.

Recall our definition of trust: *A firm belief in the character, competence and consistency of someone or something to deliver an expected result or outcome.*

When we place our trust in others, what we are doing is taking a risk that the other person has the character, competence, and consistency to complete a task and deliver on the result or outcome we expect.

When we place our trust in others, especially in situations where, if that trust is breached, it could have serious and negative implications for ourselves and/or for others, the risk to trust others can take a fair bit of courage.

At first it might seem slightly over-dramatic to say it can take courage to trust others, because for most of us, when we think of courage, we think of examples where a person or people have put themselves in danger and have overcome almost insurmountable obstacles to achieve some outstanding result … saved-the-world type of courage.

The reality is, however, courage is a virtue that most, if not all, of us possess and use almost every day of our lives.

Think about it for a moment and you will quickly realise this is true for you too.

Throughout your typical day, you might need a bit of courage to have that important conversation with someone. You'll need the courage because there's a risk that you could offend the other person, they could become defensive, they could misinterpret your intention and a host of other reasons why the conversation is important, but risky.

Throughout your typical day, you might need to try something new and because it's something you haven't tried before, there's a risk you might fail, and you'll need a bit of courage to motivate you to complete the task.

Throughout your typical day, you will also need to place your trust in others.

In your personal life, it could be placing your trust in your husband, wife or partner, your children, your friends, or other family members. It could be placing your trust in your butcher, your hairdresser, or your doctor.

In workplace settings we are often required to place our trust in others to help us meet deadlines, complete tasks, and achieve goals. At times we will need to sum up at least a little courage to place our trust in others, because sometimes there is a real risk that the other person, either intentionally or unintentionally, could let us down in some way and breach the trust we placed in them.

Again, this type of courage that I'm referring to here isn't the save-the-world type of courage, but it is nonetheless courage, and it's something we can admire in ourselves when we put it into practice, and it's certainly something other people find admirable when they see it is a virtue that we put into practice as well.

Psychologist Dr Melanie Greenberg agrees that courage is an admirable virtue, saying courage is "an attribute of good character that makes us worthy of respect".[114]

Based on her research, Greenberg suggests there are six attributes of courage, which I have listed below and highlighted how each of them can relate to the risk involved and courage we require to trust others:

1. **Feeling fear yet choosing to act:** When you are apprehensive or even feel a sense of fear to place your trust in another person because you're not completely sure if they have the character, competence or consistency to deliver the result you're expecting, there's a risk involved, and this is why it takes at least a little courage to place your trust in that person.

2. **Following your heart:** Sometimes you might choose to place your trust in another person, simply because you're following your heart or, said another way, you're courageously trusting your own gut instinct about the person's character, competency or consistency to deliver on the results you're expecting.

3. **Persevering in the face of adversity:** At times, when you might have been let down by another person, and their actions have created a difficult situation for you, it takes courage to trust that the other person won't let you down again.

4. **Standing up for what is right:** When you're personally stepping up and calling out moral, ethical or legal breaches, you'll often need to rely on others, and you'll need to have the courage to trust in them to back you up and support you in your stance.

5. **Expanding your horizons: letting go of the familiar:** Earlier in the book I shared with you my experience of tandem skydiving. The trust I had to place in my 'buddy', who I was strapped to and plunged out of the plane with, certainly took a bit of courage (or maybe stupidity). In any venture where you're about to try something new, where there is a risk, and

especially when your success depends on someone else's help, you will need to draw on your courage to trust in that person (and yourself) to achieve the result you're expecting.

6. **Facing suffering with dignity:** When life has dealt you a bad set of cards, and you're experiencing an emotionally or physically challenging reality, you'll often need to draw on your own confidence and control of self-trust, but also the courage to be supported by others, to place your trust in them at your most vulnerable times, that they will be there to support you.

So, it does take courage to trust others, to take the risk that the person in whom you are placing your trust will in fact deliver the result you expect will be achieved.

In our Triangle of Three Trusts, the lens of trust others has both the elements of courage and collaboration.

As mentioned earlier, one of the most common occasions in which we will need to place our trust in others is in the workplace. This is where the collaboration element of trust others is most evident.

In a report on 'The Collaborative Economy', global consulting firm Deloitte defines collaboration as "employees communicating and working together, building on each other's ideas to produce something new or do something differently".[115]

Often at work we need to collaborate with other people – whether that's within our own work team, or a person in a different section or department, or a person who works for another company supplying goods or services or support to you and your co-workers.

For collaboration to be successful, there must be trust by and in everybody who is involved in the collaborative effort.

While that may be stating the obvious, the reality about trust and collaboration in the workplace is not all that rosy.

For example, a study focusing on the state of collaboration in workplaces, completed by technology company Cisco, reports that 86 per cent of businesses identify collaborative and flexible teams as key to the success of their organisation, and yet 67 per cent of those surveyed have communication issues with colleagues, suppliers, and other businesses.[116]

In the Deloitte report mentioned above, their findings suggest that when employees collaborate:

- **they work 15 per cent faster, on average**
- **73 per cent do better work**
- **60 per cent are innovative**
- **56 per cent are more satisfied.**

There is no doubt then that collaboration is important to business success, and technology is certainly playing its part in developing and providing business leaders and their employees with technology-based collaborative tools.

In a 2020 *Washington Post* 'Opinion' article, Rahm Emanuel reflects on a time when he served as chief of staff for President Barack Obama, and writes this: "The United States was careening toward a global depression … and in those dark days, I uttered a phrase that's followed me ever since: 'Never allow a good crisis go to waste. It's an opportunity to do the things you once thought were impossible'".[117]

During the coronavirus pandemic, many workers were encouraged or required to work from home.

While 'distributed' or 'remote' working has been increasing over the past few decades, especially in the technology sector, this 'forced' new way of work across a range of other sectors is being seen as an opportunity for both business leaders and their teams.

As Alex Hern reported in *The Guardian*, "many employees for companies who have sent all staff home are already starting to question why they had to go into the office in the first place".[118]

With a larger number of employees now working remotely, the result has been a dramatic increase in the need for workers to communicate and collaborate using online platforms including Zoom, GoToMeeting, Webex, Microsoft Teams, and a host of other platforms and online communications software.

However, underpinning the success of people using these collaborative tools effectively is a combination of their competence in using the tools and, importantly, the trust they have in the other people with whom they are collaborating.

In the 2020 'Global Work-from-Home Experience Survey' report produced by Global Workplace Analytics, a leading authority on the future of work, CEO Kate Lister, highlights: "A key to operating in a successful work-from-home program is trust".[119]

When we consider the importance of being able to trust others, especially in this new world of working remotely, the employees need to trust each other and also, importantly, the managers need to trust their employees.

The opportunity that has arisen from this forced remote-working experience because of the Covid-19 pandemic has seen managers and their teams needing to pivot the way they work and learn.

Kate Lister highlights that the 2020 'Global Work-from-Home Experience Survey' report suggests that "Managers who have worked from home are more likely to trust that employees are being productive when working remotely".

So the experience that many senior, middle and front-line leaders across the globe have gained from being required to work remotely themselves, is resulting in an increased level of trust in their employees to be working productively – even when not in the office.

This takes us back to a point I made earlier in this chapter, which I will repeat here: Our individual and collective experiences help us to form opinions about who we think we can and cannot trust.

If leaders have personally experienced that they can be productive while working remotely, that experience will help them form the opinion that their individual and collective team members could also be trusted to productively work remotely.

This point is true in both traditional 'at-work' situations as well as 'remote-work' situations.

For us to trust others does take courage, because there is always a risk that our assessment of the other person's character, competence and consistency to complete a task and deliver on the result or outcome we expect may not be correct.

For us to place our trust in others does require collaboration – the person we are trusting needs to collaborate with us to achieve the goals we mutually have agreed on. And that person requires us to collaborate with them in ways that show we are supporting them and trusting them to get the job done.

And again, we form these opinions on whether to trust others based on our experiences as well as on what we have consciously thought about their competency, character, and consistency to deliver and achieve the results we expect. We can also base our decision to trust others on our gut feelings.

Yes … to trust others takes courage and it takes collaboration, and this is certainly the case with anyone who hops in the driver's seat next to my good friend John Doble.

As a champion rally-car navigator, John is a three times winner of the Australasian Safari alongside champion rally-car driver Steve Riley.

As I began writing this chapter, and thinking about the lens of trust others, I thought the partnership between a rally-car navigator and driver would be a great example to explore.

When you speak to John about rally-car racing and his role as navigator, there is an obvious passion in what he does.

His journey to becoming a champion rally-car navigator started when a friend of his wife, Sue, gave him a Sony PlayStation that had a game called the 'Colin McRae Rally'.

From playing that game, John's interest in rally-car racing was born … so if you are a parent worrying about the time your child is investing in online gaming … who knows where it might lead them.

The universe can certainly work in mysterious ways, and with his new-found interest in rally-car racing (at least on a video game), John discovered in a casual conversation with Gary, his manager at the time, that Gary was about to head off to compete in a car rally and his navigator had to pull out of the race.

John's manager paused for a moment, and looking at John with a wry smile, said, "And I reckon you can take his place".

So, with that, John had a couple of weeks to learn as much about navigating as he could.

They entered the race and – while this would be a much better story if they had won – unfortunately, two days into the rally they rolled the car and were out of the race.

When I asked John who was at fault to cause the crash, he figured it was a number of things, including the event navigation notes listing what was a sharp right turn as a slight right turn, the speed that Gary entered the corner, based on that advice, and the condition of the road.

As I listened to John reflect on the cause of the crash, his commitment as a team player was obvious – not finding blame, just stating things as they were.

What was evident, though, was that despite the crash, John's passion for rally-car racing was well and truly ignited.

Recognising John had a bit of potential as a navigator, Gary introduced John to a few other drivers, with whom John navigated over the next few years, which set the foundation, as John puts it, for "really learning my craft as a navigator and rally car racing project manager".

While reading what had become his favourite magazine, *Motor Sport News*, John saw an advertisement by the Steve Riley Racing Team seeking a skilled navigator to enter the Australasian Car Rally championship.

John immediately called and, after a few more phone meetings with Steve Riley, they met in person and John joined the team as navigator.

Again, this would be a better story if I could tell you that John and Steve won their first race.

Unfortunately, while they were in fact leading the race on the last day of the championship, while crossing a river (no they weren't taking a short cut), the engine took on water and they were out of the race.

The good news is, Steve and John had formed this wonderful partnership and entered again the following year and won the event … which they also won another two times as well.

Throughout my conversation with John regarding his partnership with Steve, trust was of course a central theme.

As a rally-car navigator, John had to trust the navigation notes that he and all the other navigators in the race were given prior to the race. John needed to be able to trust Steve to follow his instructions as he called them. They both needed to trust that their mechanics had the car in top condition for each race.

Steve of course needed to trust that John was calling the navigation notes at precisely the right time for him to be able to apply his own driving skills to ensure their safety, while pushing the limits to try and win the race as well.

John also shared that prior to navigating with Steve, he had occasionally navigated for one or two other drivers who were very skilled at driving, but especially when under real pressure of rally driving, would get angry, yell and swear at John.

If you knew John, getting angry and yelling just isn't his personality, and not aligned with his values.

John shared this important insight about trust when he said, "Under pressure people's personalities are amplified" and when it came to trusting those few drivers to the point of wanting to race with them again, John's decision was to part ways.

Let's take a moment to consider what you have just learned about my good friend John and how his experiences relate to the dimensions in our Triangle of Three Trusts.

There was the confidence and control that both John and Steve required for their own self-trust and, importantly, there was the obvious courage and collaboration they both required for them to trust each other.

Lastly, there was the combined character, competence, and consistency required for them to earn each other's trust.

By way of summarising this chapter on the lens of trust others, whenever we do decide to place our trust in others (or not), we are assessing whether to trust the other person based on what we think and how we feel about their combined character, competence, and consistency to deliver the result that we expect.

Which now moves us onto the next chapter – the lens of earning others' trust and the combined character, competence, and consistency required for us to demonstrate our trustworthiness.

Chapter Eight Summary

It takes both courage and collaboration to place our trust in other people. Courage because there's a risk that the other person may let us down. Collaboration because when we do place our trust in others, we have the responsibility for holding the other person accountable for our trust. Trusting others blindly is a recipe for failure.

"Connecting with others in a way that makes them feel understood and valued is key to life and the basis of building trust and loyalty."

Dr Henry Cloud

Chapter Nine

The character, competence, and consistency to earn others' trust

The Triangle of Three Trusts™

Throughout this book we have concentrated on what it means to trust ... to trust ourselves and to trust others.

In this chapter we get to what living in the light of day is really all about – the character, competence, and consistency each of us requires to earn others' trust.

Put another way, this chapter is all about trustworthiness.

The *Cambridge Dictionary* defines the word worthy as "deserving respect, admiration, or support". However, this only leads us to the question, 'What is it that makes one "deserving" of respect, admiration, or support?' … or, more to our focus here, 'What is it that makes one deserving of trust – trust*worthiness*?'

So far in exploring what it means to trust we have looked through two of three lenses. The first lens is your confidence and control required for self-trust. Through this lens you have the capacity to understand and accept your own imperfections, and your opportunity to strive and hold yourself accountable and responsible to be the best version of you.

The second lens is your courage and collaboration required to trust others. Through this lens you have the capacity to courageously take the risks to engage with others in meaningful ways to build collaborative, trust-based relationships to achieve mutually beneficial results and value.

Through all of my research to date, and everything I've written so far in this book, when it comes to living in the light of day, in genuinely striving to be the best version of you and to maximise your opportunities to live a meaningful, flourishing, and prosperous life, it is your capacity to earn others' trust, your capacity for trustworthiness, that will reap you the greatest rewards in your professional and personal life.

Let's start with the first element required to earn others' trust … character.

You have already read that one of my favourite philosophers is Aristotle, and even though his philosophy dates back some 2,500 years, there's something very 'current' in the importance he places on our capacity to flourish in this life being based on our character.

The study of character stretches across philosophical, psychological, behavioural, socio-political, religious, and economical disciplines. Which simply goes to show that it is something important in our lives.

Typically, most people think of character in terms of someone being of 'good' character or 'bad' character. Another line of considering character is to think of having 'good' character traits – like honesty, compassion, justice, gratitude, and forgiveness – or having 'bad' character traits – like dishonesty, cold-heartedness, injustice, ungratefulness, and resentfulness.

One of the most exciting research projects in the field of positive psychology was an extensive project undertaken two decades ago. A team of over 50 leading scientists collaborated over a period of three years to research globally what were the core characteristics of virtuous and positive human qualities identified over a period spanning the previous 2500 years, in philosophy, virtue ethics, moral education, psychology, and theology.[120]

After rigorous application of a range of research methodologies, this project arrived at what is now known as the *Values in Action (VIA) Classification of Character Strengths and Virtues*,[121] which has become one of the most researched areas in the field of applied positive psychology.

The original project determined that there were 24 character strengths that can be classified into six overarching virtues. Below is a summary of the six virtues and their associated character strengths:

- **The virtue of *wisdom* is demonstrated through the application of the character strengths creativity, curiosity, judgment, love of learning, and perspective.**

- **The virtue of *courage* is demonstrated through the application of the character strengths bravery, perseverance, honesty, and zest.**

- **The virtue of *humanity* is demonstrated through the application of the character strengths love, kindness, and social (or emotional) intelligence.**

- **The virtue of *justice* is demonstrated through the application of the character strengths teamwork, fairness, and leadership.**

- **The virtue of *temperance* is demonstrated through the application of the character strengths forgiveness, humility, prudence, and self-regulation.**

- **The virtue of *transcendence* is demonstrated through the application of the character strengths appreciation of beauty and excellence, gratitude, hope, humour, and spirituality.**

As you read through this VIA Classification of Character Strengths and Virtues, I am sure that some of the strengths will seem more meaningful and resonate more with you than others.

In fact, why not take a moment to read through the 24-character strengths again (don't be too concerned with the overarching six core virtues at this stage) and highlight or circle the ones that resonate most to you.

Now, return to the work you did in chapter seven on Self-trust and compare what you arrived at as your core values and character strengths with what you have highlighted or circled here.

While we could go into an academic exploration of the differences between virtues, values, principles, and character strengths here, I would rather keep it much more practical, and I am sure you would prefer that too.

As a result of the original project on the VIA Classification, the lead researchers, along with support from the philanthropic Manuel D. and Rhoda Mayerson Foundation,[122] founded what is now known as the VIA Institute on Character.[123]

If you visit the site **https://www.viacharacter.org/** you can take a free VIA survey that will provide you with a summary of the 24 character strengths, ranked by your answers on how you wish to be living your life. There is also a paid version that provides you with a more extensive and personalised report, with suggested actions and ways to practically apply the results of your VIA character strengths ... and I highly recommend you consider doing this.

Earlier in chapter seven on self-trust, we explored several ways for you to think about and determine what your core values in life are. Being able to clearly articulate them and hold yourself accountable for living up to them in your professional and personal life is key to living in the light of day, striving to be the best version of yourself, and giving yourself the best opportunity to live a meaningful, flourishing, and prosperous life.

As I shared with you in chapter seven, during my own process of determining my core values I arrived at these five: vitality (which included being present and staying healthy); contribution (which included contributing professionally and personally to making life better in some way for others); authenticity (living true to my values, especially when under stress or pressure); learning (continuing to seek wisdom and find ways to practically apply it and share it in professional and personal settings); and love (recognising and valuing the important relationships in my personal and professional life).

Again, just by way of sharing my own experience here, when I completed the VIA survey the results were very aligned with my earlier work on my values. The findings of my VIA survey showed my five top-ranked character strengths (they refer to these as 'signature strengths') are: love of learning, love, hope, honesty, and zest.

While slightly different to my earlier work, you can see there is certainly an alignment:

Core values I determined (chapter 7)	VIA character strengths
Vitality	Zest and hope
Authenticity	Honesty
Contribution	Love
Learning	Love of learning
Love	Love

I don't share this with you for my own entertainment and gratification, but rather to demonstrate how you too can apply these ideas and activities in a practical way for yourself.

There are several key points about character and character strengths that I would like to summarise here, before we move onto the other core elements of earning others' trust (competency and consistency):

Character is plural

What I mean by this is that your character as an individual is made up of and demonstrated by your 'values in action'

– in other words, the character strengths you regularly demonstrate through your words and actions represent a summary of your personal character.

I remind you once again here of the words of Aristotle: "Your actions and behaviours are your morals shown in conduct".

I personally find it kind of cool that the evidence-based research, some 2500 years since Aristotle penned those words, is validating his philosophy in this fast-paced, always-switched-on, technically driven world that is so different in so many ways from the world as it was for Aristotle.

Character strengths can be weaknesses

Any character strength applied in ways to make life better for yourself and for others can also be applied in ways that are detrimental to yourself and others.

Returning to Aristotle, he suggested that the virtuous person found the "mean in all things relative to us".[124] What this means is any character strength we might have, for example courage, if it is deficient in us it could lead to cowardice; and if it is applied in excess by us it could lead to foolhardiness. Courage is the 'mean' (or balance) between foolhardiness and cowardice.

So, as you think about your character strengths and values, think carefully about when you are applying them in a balanced and positive way, and when you might be applying them deficiently or excessively and what impact that might be having on you and on others.

Understanding your character strengths matters

In any given situation you will be using one or more of your character strengths to a higher or lesser degree.

However, what is most important from the evidence-based research is that just knowing what your character strengths are, especially what your top (or signature) strengths are, will help you to be living in the light of day, strive to be the best version of yourself and live a more meaningful, flourishing, and prosperous life.

When it comes to earning others' trust, the reality is that while character is an essential element in what it takes to be worthy of others' trust … to be trustworthy – by itself character is not enough.

You could be a person who exhibits character strengths, virtues and values in action that other people may find admirable and even aspirational; however, if they don't perceive and believe you have or are demonstrating the competence they require of you to do what they need you to do, or to be who they need you to be, they won't trust you.

For example, in a personal-life setting, you might show the character strengths and competence a person requires of you to babysit their children, and if that was what they were after, you would more than likely be in a position where they would determine you to be trustworthy.

However, even if you showed character strengths of integrity and honesty (for example) but lacked the competence to drive a car, they wouldn't trust you to pick up their children and drive them home from their school.

In a workplace setting the same applies.

At work your team members or manager might consider you to be a person who demonstrates 'good' character; however, if you lack the competence, experience or resources to perform a certain task, they may find it hard to take the risk of trusting you in that situation.

Trust, as we have covered earlier in this book, is contextual ... it depends on the person and it depends on their character and it depends on their competence.

What then is competence?

In practical terms, your competence is the combination of your skills (the things you can do), your knowledge (the things you know), your attributes (the other qualities you bring to any relationship or situation), and your experiences (the things you have done in your life).

However, when others are assessing your competence to perform a task, they might also include in their assessment the following:

- **If you don't have the skill, knowledge, attributes or experience in a certain area, do they believe you have the capacity and motivation to learn this skill and gain the experience quickly enough for them to trust you?**

- **If you don't have the skill, knowledge, attributes, or experience in a certain area, do they believe you have the resources upon which you can draw to complete the task?**

So, competence isn't just about your skill, knowledge, attributes, and experience. Competence is also about your resources and resourcefulness that will contribute to you being able to earn others' trust.

Just as a reminder here, too, your competence is not only a key element to earn others' trust, it is also, as I introduced you to in the second chapter, one of the three core elements or innate drives identified in Deci's and Ryan's Self-Determination Theory (SDT). Your competence is essential for you to tap into your internal or intrinsic motivation. (You might recall the other two core elements essential to being intrinsically motivated are relationships and autonomy).

Competence is of course contextual, which means you may have competence in certain areas and be lacking it in others.

What is essential, of course, is to determine whether you are competent in the areas you need or want to be … not only to earn others' trust, but also to achieve the personal and professional goals you're setting, to continue to learn, grow and be striving toward being your best version of you.

A competency audit

My recommendation here is that you take some time to:

1. List your various personal and professional life roles.

2. Ask yourself, if you were a professional life-coach, what would you list as the core competences required of a person to be at their best in each of those life roles.

3. Then, being as honest as you can be, give yourself a ranking in each of the competencies, using a scale of 1 being a low score and 5 being a high score.

4. Next, identify from your rankings where you are currently demonstrating high competence and be grateful for that, and focus as much as you can on applying that competence to your very best.

5. Now, take a moment to think about and take a note of the potential impact on your life and others, through your various life roles, that developing your competence in other areas might have.

6. Finally, develop a plan, set some goals around how you might enhance your competencies in the areas you have identified.

Remember, if we are not learning and growing, it is easy to start to stagnate and languish ... and that's certainly not living in the light of day, not striving to be the best version of you, and not living a meaningful, flourishing, and prosperous life.

Taking stock of where we are up to in this chapter on earning others' trust, we have explored how your character and your competence contribute to other people determining your trustworthiness.

However, the research confirms that there is a third area required to combine with your character and competence to be trustworthy: consistency.

Have you ever known someone who can at times demonstrate the elements of 'good' character and who has the competence required to do their job or complete a task effectively and efficiently, and yet – perhaps it is when they are under pressure, or for some other reason – they show inconsistencies in either their 'good' character or their competence?

Think back to the second chapter of this book where we explored (arguably) good people committing intentional acts of deception.

Trust is earned and, over time, a person's trustworthiness becomes even more apparent.

Remember one of the overarching principles of this book is this: People WILL get your truth: *Over time, your intentions, promises, actions and results will either promote you as trustworthy or expose you as not.*

Look again at our Triangle of Three Trusts. Notice how the arrows lead up from self-trust toward earn others' trust. This is an intentional element in the model to reflect this point:

When we demonstrate in our words, actions, and results that we have the 'control' (self-discipline, self-awareness, self-control, self-accountability) that is required of us for

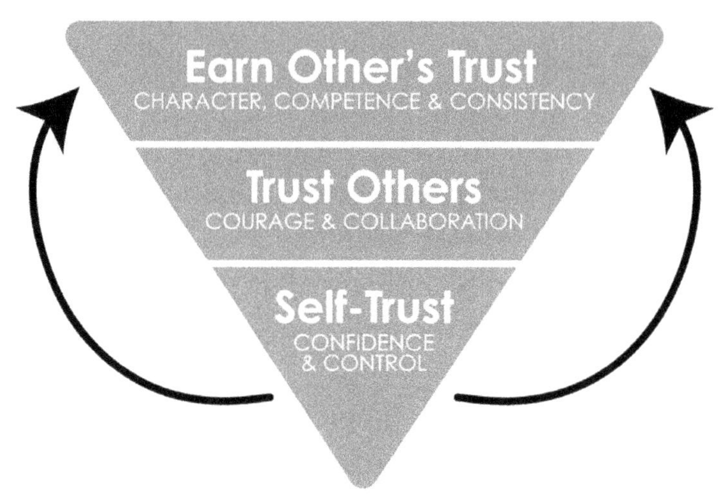

The Triangle of Three Trusts™

true self-trust, this becomes our self-control mechanism for the consistency required in demonstrating our character and competence in ways that help people determine our trustworthiness – our capacity to earn others' trust.

In other words, without continuing work on our own self-trust, striving to be the best version of ourselves and living in the light of day, we will potentially lack consistency in demonstrating our 'good' character and competence in moments that matter … and that puts earning others' trust at risk.

This concludes our exploration of the three lenses of trust – the confidence and control required for self-trust; the courage and collaboration required to trust in others;

and the character, competence, and consistency required to earn others' trust.

I hope that by using these three lenses you can explore ways to earn, build, and maintain more trust in your professional and personal life.

In the next chapter I want to share with you some of the latest in evidence-based research and practical strategies from my field of positive psychology, on what science has uncovered can help you, me and others flourish – even in tough times.

While there have been many books – both academic and more self-help focused – that cover the broad topics that sit in and around positive psychology, I want to share with you what I have personally found to be the most significant, meaningful, and practical research and strategies that can help us all build character, earn trust and act with integrity, so that we can strive to be at our personal best and live more meaningful, flourishing, and prosperous lives.

Chapter Nine Summary

Looking at life through a lens of Earning Others' Trust helps to confirm we need to have 'good' character, appropriate competence and consistently demonstrate our intentional striving to act with good character and competence in all that we do. Choosing to strive to be the best version of you will help you earn others' trust and live a more meaningful, flourishing, and prosperous life.

"The best teacher both in art and science is the experience."

Miguel de Cervantes

Chapter Ten

A meaningful, flourishing, and prosperous life

I don't know what the meaning of life is ... that's a question I will leave for others. In fact, I personally think the more valuable question is 'How do we live a meaningful life?'

I really like the word 'meaningful' in this question and context ... How do we live a life *full of meaning* – a meaning-full life?

It is through our relationships that many of us find meaning in our lives – our relationships are one of the core elements that contribute to us living a meaning-full life.

In chapter three I introduced you to the science of intention and the evidence-based research that demonstrates how our intentions directly impact our relationships.

You learned that an applied positive intention is any action based on a mindful awareness of *why* you are going to do *what* you are going to do and the *impact* it will have on others.

Through this altruistic approach to life, in wanting to mindfully and intentionally make life better for others, we create value for others, and in so doing, typically will receive value back for ourselves.

This evidence-based realisation, that there is a *creation of value through our applied positive intentions, is what I refer to as Intentionomics®.*

My definition of Intentionomics® is *'the individual and collective impact of our intentions on ourselves and on others'.*

One of my favourite quotes is from the amazing anthropologist and primatologist Jane Goodall, who said this:

> *"You cannot get through a single day without having an impact on the world around you. What you do makes a difference, and you have to decide what kind of difference you want to make".*

Each of us has the opportunity to decide on what kind of difference we want to make through our intentional actions ... it is this decision that will reflect on the kind of person we want to be and the type of life we want to lead.

In essence, I have written *Living in the Light of Day* to help you, me and everyone else explore what it means to live a 'good life' – a life where you can build your character, earn trust, and act with integrity.

But what does it mean to live a 'good life' and what are the elements that contribute to human flourishing?

Researchers across fields including psychology, sociology, economics, and philosophy have been exploring these questions for many hundreds of years.

However, it was during his 1998 American Psychology Association (APA) presidential address that Dr Martin Seligman strongly advocated for the profession of psychology to not only focus on mental illness, but to also extend its research into the elements that contribute to a flourishing life.

In Seligman's words, "Psychology is not just the study of weakness and damage; it is also the study of strength and virtue. Treatment is not just fixing what is broken; it is nurturing what is best within us".[125]

So was born the field of *positive psychology*, and while there are differing definitions of the goal of positive psychology, the two that I find most helpful are (1) to increase human flourishing[126] and (2) to help change people's wellbeing for the better.[127]

If you were to ask most parents what they want for their children in life, you won't hear many of them answer with "I want them to flourish" or "I want them to maximise their wellbeing".

What you will typically hear is something similar to "I just want them to be happy".

I know from all the research I have undertaken, both academically and experientially, especially in the fields of philosophy, ethics and applied positive psychology, that happiness is most certainly not the only thing in life we ought to be pursuing.

However, like so many other parents when asked what they want for their children, Liz and I typically respond with – "We just want them to be happy".

This is not to say that we don't want our children to feel and experience other emotions … I hope they feel sadness when a friend or family member is unwell or dies; I hope they feel anger at injustices they experience or see; I hope they feel frustration when things don't always work out exactly how they want them to; I hope they feel wonder and awe at the magnificence of nature and human endeavour … and the list goes on.

Yes, I want them to be happy most of the time, but I certainly don't want them to only feel happiness.

Here's the thing, though: Happiness is so subjective and contextual, and to make matters more confusing, academics and researchers cannot agree on a definition.

In the introductory chapter of the 1097-page volume (weighing just on two kilograms) *The Oxford Handbook of Happiness*, which had 121 contributing academics, researchers and practitioners, the authors wrote this:

"For the purposes of this volume we chose to consider happiness in its broadest sense, treating it as an umbrella concept for notions such as well-being, subjective well-being, psychological well-being, hedonism, eudaimonia, health, flourishing and so on".[128]

I am not asking you to define happiness, or wellbeing or flourishing, but to think about what it means for you to have lived a life 'well lived' … to have lived a 'good life'.

The topics that positive psychology researchers are interested in studying are wide and varied; however, this is what we are mostly concerned with – the elements that contribute to us living a 'good life'.

This is why we often refer to wellbeing as *subjective wellbeing*, because how you personally perceive what it means to live a good life can be quite different to how others might perceive it.

So, again, my intention in writing this chapter is to allow you to think about your own subjective wellbeing … to think about the extent to which you believe you are living a 'good life', and to help you gain clarity on what living a good life actually means for you … because again, it will mean different things to different people.

Let's start this exploration of what it means for you to live a 'good life' by using a relatively easy self-assessment tool developed by Hadley Cantril, which is commonly referred to as the Ladder of Life.[129]

Take a look at this image of a ladder, where the top rung (numbered 10) represents the best possible life for you and the bottom rung (numbered 0) represents the worst possible life for you. What number rung of the ladder would you say best represents your life at the moment?

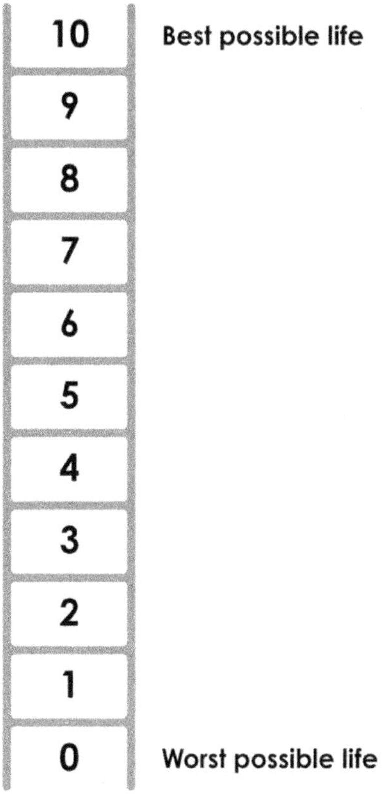

10 Best possible life
9
8
7
6
5
4
3
2
1
0 Worst possible life

Cantril's "Ladder of Life"
Source: Cantril, H. (1965)

Now that you have selected a number that represents where you currently believe you are in terms of living your best possible life, I highly recommend that you take some time to answer the following questions:

- **What are the best elements (people and things) in your life that you are grateful for right now?**

- **What would you like to have or experience that would make your life even better?**

- **What would you like *not* to have or experience that would make your life even better?**

- **How are your current decisions and actions helping you move toward your best possible life?**

- **How are your current decisions and actions hindering you from moving toward your best possible life?**

Another tool that has been used extensively by positive psychology researchers and coaches is the Satisfaction With Life Scale (SWLS).[130] It was developed by Ed Diener and his colleagues, Robert Emmons, Randy Larsen and Sharon Griffin.

Here are five statements that you may agree or disagree with. Using the 1-7 scale shown, indicate your agreement with each item by placing the appropriate number on the line preceding that item. Please be open and honest in your responding.

7-Strongly agree

6-Agree

5-Slightly agree

4-Neither agree nor disagree

3-Slightly disagree

2-Disagree

1-Strongly disagree

1. _____ In most ways my life is close to the ideal.

2. _____ The conditions of my life are excellent.

3. _____ I am satisfied with my life.

4. _____ So far, I have achieved the things I want in life.

5. _____ If I could live my life over, I would change almost nothing.

The SWLS is one of the most widely used measures of life satisfaction in the world[131] and when you add up your scores you will arrive at a number between 5 and 35.

In their book, *Happiness: Unlocking the mysteries of psychological wealth*, Ed Diener and Robert Biswas-Diener provide the following interpretation of scoring for you:

31–35: Extremely satisfied

26–30: Satisfied

21–25: Slightly satisfied

20: Neutral; an equal mix of satisfaction and dissatisfaction

15–19: Slightly dissatisfied

10-14: Dissatisfied

5–9: Extremely dissatisfied

Now that you have completed the SWLS, I recommend you return to the questions you answered after completing the Ladder of Life exercise.

Read through each of the questions and your answers and take a moment to consider whether you could change your answers in any way.

The SWLS and the Ladder of Life activities are quite broad in their approach to helping you take stock of where you are right now in terms of living a 'good life' and being the best version of yourself.

To delve a little deeper, though, we need to explore more specifically the elements that the evidence-based research tells us are the major contributors to our overall sense of wellbeing and flourishing in life.

There is always a danger in presenting a list of such elements because there will typically be someone who will put their hand up and say, "What about … "

For example:

- **Carol Ryff identified six contributing elements to flourishing: self-acceptance, positive relations with others, autonomy, environmental mastery, purpose in life, and personal growth.**[132]

- **Martin Seligman identified five contributing elements: positive emotions, engagement, relationships, meaning, and achievement.**[133]

- **Richard Ryan and Edward Deci identified three contributing elements: autonomy, competence, and relatedness.**[134]

- **Tom Rath and Jim Harter identified five contributing elements: career wellbeing, social wellbeing, financial wellbeing, physical wellbeing, and community wellbeing.**[135]

- **Paul Lawrence and Nitin Nohria identified four contributing elements: our drives to acquire, bond, learn, and defend.**[136]

What we also know from positive psychology research is that some people report having a positive sense of wellbeing even though their objective life circumstances may be difficult, and yet others report they feel like they are languishing in their lives even though their life circumstances are very positive.

One research project undertaken to assess how people 'feel' about their overall sense of wellbeing was conducted by Felicia Huppert and Timothy So from the University of Cambridge.[137]

Huppert's and So's research covered over 46,000 adults in 23 European nations and they determined that people who had a sense of flourishing in their lives typically reported high scores in what they referred to as *core features*, which were: (1) positive emotions, (2) engagement and interest, and (3) meaning and purpose.

Their findings also suggested that to have a sense of flourishing in life, in addition to reporting all three of the 'core features', respondents needed to have high scores in at least three of what they referred to as *additional features*: self-esteem, optimism, resilience, vitality, self-determination, and positive relationships.

We can add to the list other elements across a range of academic, psychological, and philosophical fields such as our sense of curiosity, willpower, mindfulness, gratitude, integrity, trust, virtues, values, and character strengths.

So where does this leave us, when different researchers claim different elements contribute to our sense of flourishing, and some of them will have more impact than others?

IT'S UP TO YOU!

It means only you can really determine whether you're living in the light of day and strive to be the best version of yourself.

What I've found personally helpful, and have been successfully applying with my executive coaching clients for many years now, is to start with the two activities that you have already completed earlier in this chapter – Cantril's Ladder of Life and the Satisfaction With Life Scale (SWLS).

However, while each of these draws a line in the sand on your overall assessment of how well you are living a meaningful, flourishing and prosperous life, they don't really provide much help on areas you might want to work on, do more of, or develop.

That's why I have selected from the vast research on what science tells us contributes to our subjective well-being and our overall sense of life satisfaction, and have developed the 25 Contributing Elements to Living a Good Life Questionnaire and Implementation Plan.

This is not a psychological self-assessment to measure your overall sense of wellbeing or flourishing; rather it is a self-reflection and development tool to get you thinking about a range of elements that can contribute to your overall sense of life satisfaction.

There is, however, a rating scale that I recommend you use. It is just a way for you to think about each element, and to choose what best reflects the extent to which you believe that element is contributing to your current sense of life satisfaction.

For each of the contributing elements I will provide a brief description, then the scale for you to give yourself a 'rating', an evidence-based positive psychology activity that you can apply, and evidence of what you will experience as you complete the activity.

Here is the rating scale:

Never – This is something I never experience in my life.

Rarely – This is something I rarely experience in my life.

Occasionally – This is something I occasionally experience in my life.

Often – This is something I often experience in my life.

Consistently – This is something I consistently experience in my life.

25 contributing elements to living a good life questionnaire and implementation plan

Here is a list of 25 contributing elements to living a good life and on the following pages, you will be able to reflect and consider how important each is to you and I will provide you with some guidance on how you can personally benefit from experiencing them.

Again, as I highlighted earlier, I am not suggesting this list of 25 contributing elements to living a good life is a complete list. As you read through the list and complete the questionnaire and implementation plan, you might think of others to add to the list, and I encourage you to do so.

1. Emotional agility

This includes your overall sense of positivity in your life as well as your capacity to choose and manage appropriate emotions in both positive and challenging situations.

Never | Rare | Occasionally | Often | Consistently

Context: This is not about positive thinking or just looking at the world through rose-coloured glasses. You've read earlier that the reality is, life isn't easy, and there are difficult times we all experience.

Key point: The key here is to be aware that you are not your thoughts and you are not your emotions – and that you can take positive goal-supportive action guided by your values – regardless of what you think or how you feel.

Activity: To prove to yourself that regardless of your thoughts or feelings you can take positive goal-supportive action guided by your values, tell yourself you are *not* going to do something (for example, "I'm not going to go for a walk" or "I can't do five more push-ups" or "I'm not going to just sit and breathe silently to myself for one minute" or "I'm not going to do any of these things" … and do them anyway.

Evidence: If you attempt any of the above, and actually do what you tell yourself you can't or won't, you have proven you are not your thoughts or feelings, and that you can choose goal-supportive action guided by your values, regardless of what you think or feel.

2. Mindful engagement

This includes applying your character strengths and competencies in activities that boost your vitality, meaning, and wellbeing.

Never | Rarely | Occasionally | Often | Consistently

Context: When we engage in activities that challenge us to use our competencies and character strengths, we get a boost in our physical and psychological wellbeing.

Key point: When we are not regularly, intentionally, and consciously applying our competencies and character strengths, we feel a sense that something is missing in our lives.

Activity: If you haven't already completed the online free Values in Action (VIA) Character Strengths questionnaire at www.viacharacter.org I recommend you do so. Then, select one of your top three character strengths and over the next week choose an activity that you haven't done for some time that involves using that character strength.

Evidence: As you do the activity, you will prove to yourself that when you're applying your competence and character strengths, you get a boost in your sense of vitality and wellbeing.

3. Supportive relationships

This includes the clarity you have on your intentions for others – what you want *for* them, not just what you want from them, and an awareness of the impact of your intentions and actions on yourself and on others.

Never | Rarely | Occasionally | Often | Consistently

Context: Much of this book has been about the importance of positive and supportive relationships in your life, and very little in life can be achieved without them.

Key point: Your relationships with yourself and with other people are based on trust. The foundation upon which trust stands is your intention for the other person in the relationship (or if the relationship is with yourself, then it's based on your intention for yourself). And your intention is being clear about and taking action on what you want *for* the other person, and not just what you want from them.

Activity: Return to the exercise you have already completed in this book on writing out an Applied Positive Intention for someone in your personal or professional life. What do you want *for* them – not what do you want *from* them? Then have a conversation with that person to check that what you want for them is what they expect from you.

Evidence: As you complete the activity, you are choosing to apply an altruistic way of making life better for others. Not only will you see the positive impact on the other person when you do something *for* them that makes their life better in some way, you will notice how positive the activity is for you … that's reciprocity – what you give out you get back.

4. A sense of meaning in life

This includes an understanding of and taking action on what brings meaning to your life.

Never | Rarely | Occasionally | Often | Consistently

Context: There are many ways people can derive a sense of meaning in their lives – it could be through relationships, religion, charity work, accepting difficult situations they have no control over, or striving to improve or achieve something in their personal or professional life, just to name a few.

Key point: Unless we know what brings meaning into our life, or what gives us a sense of living a meaningful life, we can fall into the trap of feeling that life has no meaning or is meaningless rather than meaningful.

Activity: This activity is known as 'expressive writing' and involves writing (typing) in detail about what and why certain things are important to you in your life. Choose either your personal or professional life (or you could choose both), and write in detail about the people, things, and experiences you have that are important to you. As you write down something, explain in writing why that something or someone is important to you. Go into as much detail and description as you can. Also think about and write down a lesson that you have learned or are learning either from the person, thing, or experience, or even from the activity of writing about them.

Evidence: If you have ever watched a friend or family member recount an important and positive (or meaningful) experience, you will notice how their energy levels increase, their posture changes, their eyes widen, and they become deeply engaged in the recounting of the experience, as if they were right there in that moment again. That's what you will typically experience from this exercise. You'll notice physical and emotional energy shifts in yourself – smiling as you write, as well as maybe being a little sad as you write (meaning and purpose in life are often experienced through sadness and striving through struggle, not only through experiencing 'good times').

5. Personal growth and accomplishment

This includes a commitment to life-long learning and the application of your competencies to make life better for yourself and for others.

Never | Rarely | Occasionally | Often | Consistently

Context: Personal growth and achievement are intertwined with so many other contributing elements to living a good life. If we are not learning, we are not growing, and if we are not growing, we can quickly start to languish and not have that sense of achievement that is so important to us flourishing in life.

Key point: We often move quickly from day to day and week to week, ready to start whatever is next in our lives. The problem is, most of us achieve both small and big things in our lives more often than we realise, and we often forget to look back and reflect on what we have achieved.

Activity: Take a moment at the end of this week and reflect on (a) a small or large achievement you have accomplished in your professional or personal life, and (b) what you have learned or re-learned that will help you strive to be the best version of yourself and live a good life.

Evidence: Having a sense of achievement is associated with higher reported levels of well-being. When we reflect on our achievements, even the smaller ones, we add to our sense of engagement and meaningfulness, upon which helps build our resilience in tough times.

6. A sense of autonomy

This includes your sense of what you can and cannot control in your life, and your personal accountability for the decisions you make and actions you take.

Never | Rarely | Occasionally | Often | Consistently

Context: Your sense of autonomy is one of the three innate drives that develop your sense of self-determination, which is key to tapping into and releasing your internal or intrinsic motivation (the other two being your sense of competence and your sense of relatedness).

Key point: Your sense of autonomy is not about how comfortable you are with being alone. As detailed earlier in the book, while understanding that we cannot control all that happens in our lives, to have a sense of our own autonomy means believing we have at least some control over our lives and, most importantly, that we have control over our own behaviour.

Activity: This week, to reinforce your sense of autonomy and that you are in control of your choices and decisions, make some choices that are different to what you might normally choose. An example might be to choose to cook something that you wouldn't normally cook, or to take a route to work that you wouldn't normally take.

Evidence: As you make different but deliberate and intentional choices this week, notice how you feel at the point of making the decision or taking the action. Typically, you will feel more positive about life, more in control of your life, and more motivated to make more intentional and deliberate decisions.

7. Physical health

This includes your understanding and commitment to actions that move you continually toward a balanced and healthy lifestyle.

Never | Rarely | Occasionally | Often | Consistently

Context: Not all of us are blessed with physical health, and some of us make not-so-wise decisions that can adversely impact our physical health. Still others of us are in a very healthy physical state.

Key point: Regardless of our state of physical health, the choices we make and actions we take will impact to a greater or lesser extent our existing and future physical wellbeing.

Activity: This week choose to do something to improve your physical health. For example, it might be to choose better food and beverage options, get a little more sleep, add something new to your exercise routine, make time to learn or practise yoga and/or meditate (yes, meditation has been proven to improve physical as well as psychological wellbeing).[138]

Evidence: Most of us have experienced increased vitality, clarity of mind, and a general boost in how we feel physically (and mentally) when we exercise. If this is an activity you choose to do, you will undoubtedly be giving yourself a well-earned pat on the back for looking after yourself and doing something positive to help you strive to be the best version of you.

8. Financial health

This includes your understanding and commitment to aligning your financial and lifestyle decisions and actions to help you achieve your goals.

Never | Rarely | Occasionally | Often | Consistently

Context: Your relationship with money and the choices you make with how you earn, spend, and invest it have a direct impact on your overall sense of life satisfaction and your capacity to flourish.

In a major piece of research undertaken by Elizabeth Dunn and Michael Norton, they found using money in the following ways, is more likely to boost your sense of life satisfaction and happiness:

- **Buy Experiences: spend your money on experiences not just on more 'stuff' to keep up with the Joneses and for social comparison reasons. Their research found material things don't boost our sense of life satisfaction for long (remember the IUTI syndrome – we just get used to stuff)**

- **Make it a Treat: This is again based on the IUTI syndrome. If you spend your money on the same thing(s) all the time, you just get used to them. So cut back on some of what you typically buy, and only buy it as a treat or on special occasion.**

- **Buy Time: This is simply spending your money in outsourcing the tasks you don't enjoy, to free up your time to enjoy the things you do.**

- **Pay Now, Consume Later: In a world where most of us use our credit cards to consume now and pay later, this seems counter intuitive. However, consider the joy and positive**

expectation you get when you're planning a trip. You pay for the flights, accommodation, and tours often in advance, and their research shows this can almost be as big a boost to your happiness as the trip itself (almost).

- **Invest in Others: This may not come as much of a surprise, however their research shows spending money on others can provide a bigger happiness boost than spending money on yourself … for example when you give a friend or loved one a gift, or donate to charity.[139]**

Key point: Aligning your financial goals with your lifestyle goals means you need to have both. That is, you need to be clear about how you want to live your life, and how much money you will need to financially support that lifestyle.

Activity: An old adage of success with finances is to 'spend less than you earn'. In one report,[140] it is estimated that 86 per cent of people don't have a clue about how much they spend. This week make the commitment to start a budget by tracking every (yes, every) dollar you spend. You might want to seek professional help from an accountant or financial adviser to get your lifestyle and financial goals aligned.

Evidence: What we know from research into money and wellbeing is that once you're earning enough to cover the 'basics of living', boosts in how much you earn do not equate necessarily with boosts in your wellbeing. This is not to say money doesn't make you happy (despite this being a typical saying). What is more important, though, as highlighted above by Norton's and Dunn's research, is how you spend your money will impact your sense of wellbeing more than how much money you have.[141]

9. Optimism

This includes your sense that the future will be mostly positive.

Never | Rarely | Occasionally | Often | Consistently

Context: Optimism is quite different from positivity. Positivity or positive thinking, especially in difficult times, is almost ignoring reality and saying things are good or ok, even when they're not. Optimism, on the other hand, is a fundamental belief that the future is going to be ok – it's the classic belief that there will be a light at the end of the tunnel.

Key point: What we know from the research is that being either optimistic or positive isn't always good for you – especially if you ignore reality. For example, staying optimistic and positive about an ailment, when you might need to be checked out by a doctor, or staying positive and living in hope rather than taking appropriate action toward goal achievement are not good actions.

Activity: In his book, *Learned Optimism*,[142] Martin Seligman suggests two ways to develop more optimism in your life. The first is when you realise you are thinking negatively or pessimistically, to distract yourself with some other activity. The second is to challenge or dispute the logic or reality of the pessimistic thought. I also recommend you revisit the work you did on your personal values in chapter seven, and if you find yourself having difficult thoughts or feelings that are causing you to procrastinate, become anxious or overwhelmed, remember that a thought is just a thought and a feeling is just a feeling, and that you have total control over the actions you take – regardless of those thoughts or feelings. It's sort of like if you're feeling pessimistic, act like an optimist anyway.

Evidence: Your sense of optimism can be a bit like flexing a muscle … the more you use it the stronger it gets. As you take appropriate steps, aligned with your personal values and toward achieving goals and striving to be the best version of yourself, you just get better at doing it … you become stronger in your optimism – not ignoring the realities of life, but equipping yourself with the knowledge and capability to take control over the one thing in life you have control over – your choice of action.

10. Resilience

This includes your sense that when things don't turn out as you planned, or you encounter a difficult experience, you get back to 'normal' fairly quickly.

Never | Rarely | Occasionally | Often | Consistently

Context: While optimism is a belief that the future will be ok, resilience is the practice of using your character strengths, mindset, competencies, relationships, and values to support and guide you through tough times.

Key point: Resilience is how well a person can adapt to any difficult event in their life … and, as we've covered in this book – life isn't always easy. Resilience isn't just positive thinking or optimism or goal striving or willpower … it's drawing on a range of personal and external resources and support to help you better manage difficult times.

Activity: What we know from resilience research is that the supportive relationships you have in your life are one of the main resources that can help build resilience. This week take a moment to think about the people you can really depend on, that you are very comfortable with sharing any difficult thoughts, feelings or struggle you might have. Another key source of resilience is your own physical fitness. This week, up the intensity of your exercise routine (or start one if you're not a regular exerciser).

Evidence: What you will discover as you reflect on your supportive relationships is a sense of belonging (one of the innate drivers of all human beings), which boosts a number of 'happy' hormones including oxytocin.[143] In addition, another happy hormone you will release naturally in your body when exercising is serotonin. This natural boost in your energy and mood helps build your capacity for resilience.

11. Career

This includes your sense that your work life is mostly a positive experience.

Never | Rarely | Occasionally | Often | Consistently

Context: Not everyone has a career or professional calling or does meaningful work – work that they find full of meaning and value. However, researchers Tom Rath and Jim Harter[144] have found that whatever job we are in does impact our sense of wellbeing.

Key point: While you might not be in a job that overly excites you or that you find full of meaning in your life, what you can do is focus on the positive things that are around you at work. For example, the relationships you have, the money you earn to support your lifestyle, or a realisation that this is just a stepping stone toward something better.

Activity: This is similar to the 'gratitude exercise'. This week take a moment to write down the positive things about your work and the things that you are grateful for that you experience in your work.

Evidence: Even when we might not be experiencing meaningful work, we can still find a sense of meaning and value when we look at what is positive about the work we do. This is an expression of your sense of self-determination … that while you might not be able to control everything in your life, you can control how you choose to view it. As you focus on this approach you will experience a sense of internal motivation and a boost in your overall sense of wellbeing.

12. Community

This includes your sense that you are part of a community that is safe, satisfying, and supportive.

Never | Rarely | Occasionally | Often | Consistently

Context: We humans are at our very base 'herd animals' … meaning we have an innate drive to belong. The community we belong to and participate in can have a direct impact on our sense of wellbeing and flourishing.

Key point: Some people find meaning in the activities they become involved with in their community. Whether that's joining the parents and citizens association at their local school, belonging to community sports clubs, doing charitable work, belonging to a local church, or simply being friendly with neighbours. The key here is to find how being part of a community helps you strive to be at your best.

Activity: Choose a way in which you are already an active part of your community (or choose one that you might find rewarding) and, when you get involved, notice the impact it has on you emotionally and physically.

Evidence: Being part of your local community, in whatever way you choose, will help you form relationships, express your character strengths and competence, and these are contributing elements to living a good life that will result in you experiencing positive emotions and physical wellbeing.

13. Curiosity

This includes your sense of awe, interest, and open mindedness in whatever life presents to you. It also includes being open minded to other people's perspectives, opinions, and actions.

Never | Rarely | Occasionally | Often | Consistently

Context: One of our greatest capacities as humans is not only to be inquisitive during amazing moments in our lives, but also to enhance the more mundane parts of our lives by approaching them with an open mind and willingness to explore, learn, and grow in our knowledge, competence, and character.

Key point: When we tap into our curiosity, we can look at the world anew – it encourages us to explore our environment, discover possibilities, and grow, both personally and professionally.

Activity: This week, practise being even more curious than usual by consciously and purposefully asking yourself questions about something you would typically ignore or take for granted in your everyday life. For example, if you go for a regular daily walk, try to look for something you haven't noticed before, or pick something you always notice, but ask yourself some questions about it. For example: How long has this been here? What else does this impact? What is it about this that causes me to notice it more now? What might my noticing this tell me about myself? Don't be restricted by these questions; let your curiosity challenge you.

Evidence: While practising the activity outlined might seem a little childish, the benefits you will experience (if you have the courage to try it) can include an increased sense of cognitive awareness and vitality, an increased sense of gratitude, and an increased sense of awe and wonder. Curiosity has been shown to have five major benefits: increased health and longevity, increased cognitive (thinking) skills, increased meaning, and purpose in life, improved social relationships, and increased general happiness and wellbeing.[145]

14. Willpower and grit

This includes your sense that you have the self-control and determination to achieve your goals.

Never | Rarely | Occasionally | Often | Consistently

Context: Your willpower is like a muscle. If you don't use it enough it becomes weak, but if you are in a situation where you need to constantly use it, it can become fatigued.

Key point: In her wonderful book *The Willpower Instinct* researcher and author Kelly McGonigal makes the key point that "the best way to improve your self-control is to see how and why you lose control".[146]

Activity: This week take time to focus on one of the following:

A. an area of your life that you would like to *stop* experiencing, or experience less

B. an area of your life that you would like to *start* experiencing, or experience more

C. an area of your life that is currently at risk, but you would like to *continue* experiencing.

Once you've selected which of the above areas you're going to work on, take at least one positive action toward achieving improvement. Remember, any difficult or challenging thoughts or feelings that might pop into your head are just thoughts and feelings – they don't control you ... you have control over your actions. So, align your intentional actions with your values and take a step toward being the best version of yourself and toward living a good life.

Evidence: Just having a crack at doing many of these activities will give you a stronger sense of self-determination and achievement. Each activity demonstrates that you do have the willpower – the control over your choices of action – regardless of any difficult or challenging thoughts or feelings you might experience along the way.

15. Gratitude

This includes your sense of appreciation for all you have, rather than a focus on what you don't have, want, or need.

Never | Rarely | Occasionally | Often | Consistently

Context: Being grateful is acknowledging and being thankful for any 'good' in your life and realising that while sometimes these good things we experience are from our own actions, often they are experienced through the generous actions of others.

Key point: While being grateful is a feeling, gratitude is also something we choose to have.

Activity: Consider starting a gratitude journal, where you can get creative with words and pictures that record the 'good' in your life … the things and people and experiences for which you are grateful. Make the exercise more meaningful by not just listing what you're grateful for but taking the time to record why you're grateful.

Another activity is simply to meet with, call or write to someone you care for and let them know how grateful you are to have them in your life.

Evidence: You'll find it pretty hard not to smile and get that warm feeling and glow when you focus your mindful attention on what you're grateful for. Like so many of these activities, you'll be releasing the happy hormones in your brain that the research shows have direct benefits to your psychological and physiological wellbeing.

16. Goals

This includes your sense of striving to achieve specific aspirational things or experiences in your personal and professional life.

Never | Rarely | Occasionally | Often | Consistently

Context: As aspirational goal-seeking beings, without goals or something to be striving for, humans can feel like they're languishing – that something's missing in their lives.

Key point: Goals don't have to be 'reach for the star' type of aspirations for them to have a positive impact on your wellbeing.

Setting a daily 'to do' list and crossing off each item as you complete it can boost your sense of self-determination and achievement.

Activity: If you're not in the practice of setting a daily 'to do' list, give it a go. Think about where you are, what you've experienced so far, and what you have in your life.

While being grateful for these, get curious and think about what else you might like to have, experience, learn, or do to help you strive to be at your best and live a more meaningful, flourishing, and prosperous life.

The important part of goal setting that many people miss, is to be careful not to get caught in the success trap of social comparison.

When setting personal or professional life goals, whether short, medium or long term goals, ask yourself this: How will the pursuit and achievement of this goal help me strive to be at my best, improve the lives of those around me, and help me live an even more meaningful, flourishing and prosperous life?

Evidence: Notice the feelings of positivity and achievement when you cross off the items you complete.

17. Integrity

This includes your sense of authenticity, truthfulness, and always striving to act in alignment with your personal values.

Never | Rarely | Occasionally | Often | Consistently

Context: In his book *Integrity*,[147] Dr Henry Cloud identifies six qualities of character that define integrity. They are:

- **the ability to connect with others, earn, build, and maintain trust**
- **being a realist and understanding that life isn't always easy**
- **a focus on and track history of getting things done**
- **a realisation that life is about solving problems – and there are plenty to solve**
- **a commitment to self-improvement**
- **an awareness of and reverence to a bigger life view beyond being self-centered.**

Key point: Integrity is not one thing, it is a combination of character traits demonstrated in action and consistently throughout life.

Activity: Read through the six qualities of character above and select one to work on over the next week. Ask yourself what you could start, stop, or continue to do that will build this quality of integrity in your life.

Evidence: Integrity is a combination of character traits in action, and when you consistently demonstrate your integrity you will notice more trust will develop in your life. As you earn more trust, more opportunities for goal achievement and personal development will present themselves to you.

18. Self-trust

This includes your sense of confidence, self-compassion, and control to be the best version of yourself.

Never | Rarely | Occasionally | Often | Consistently

Context: Our sense of 'self' is one of the contributing elements upon which others will form opinions about our trustworthiness.

Key point: There is a significant difference between having a big ego and having self-trust. If we let our egos get too big, we become arrogant, and that puts trust at risk. Whereas, if our self-trust is based on our own belief in our character, competence, and consistency in behaviour, and the feedback from others, we are demonstrating our trustworthiness.

Activity: None of us is perfect. Being honest with yourself, select one habit or activity that you know is not aligned with your personal values and not moving you toward being the best version of yourself, and take action to do it less - or even better replace it with some other, more positive activity.

Evidence: As you mindfully work on your self-trust you are tapping into your sense of self-determination (your sense of autonomy, competence, and relatedness), all of which the evidence shows will release more intrinsic motivation for you to achieve more in life.

19. Trust others

This includes the sense of courage and collaboration you are willing to place in others in your professional and personal life.

Never | Rarely | Occasionally | Often | Consistently

Context: Almost everything we do in life will require us in some way to have the courage and collaboration skills to trust other people.

Key point: Blindly trusting others is fraught with danger. Hold other people to account for the trust you place in them.

Activity: When you place your trust in someone this week to get something done for you, check in with them to see what you can do to support or help them achieve whatever it is you're trusting them to do.

Evidence: When people know you trust them, and that you've got their back to support them (if needed), you are building stronger trust relationships. Paradoxically, the more you trust other people, the more trust you will see others will place in you.

20. Earn others' trust

This includes your sense of character, competence, and consistency in striving to be the best version of yourself and to be worthy of other people's trust.

Never | Rarely | Occasionally | Often | Consistently

Context: Earning others' trust is all about your trustworthiness and requires all three elements of being a person of good character, being a person who demonstrates competence, and being a person who consistently acts in ways that demonstrate character, competence, and aligned personal values.

Key point: Everyone makes mistakes; however, if you get clear on your intention for others (what you want *for* them, not what you want from them), if you do make an unintentional mistake, your character, competence, and consistency will allow others to still see you as trustworthy. (Note: Repeatedly making mistakes, even if you are clear on your intentions for others, is a demonstration that your character, competence or consistency need more work and your trustworthiness is in question).

Activity: Thinking about the three elements for trustworthiness – character, competence, and consistency – choose one element to work on this week. What could you start, stop or continue to do that will enhance this element of your trustworthiness?

Evidence: The research is clear here – relationships matter and trust is at the heart of almost all positive relationships. As you focus on your trustworthiness, you'll be building more trust-based relationships, which is one of the major sources of meaning in our lives.

21. Forgiveness

This includes your sense of understanding that none of us is perfect and that we all make mistakes – and your willingness to let bygones be bygones.

Never | Rarely | Occasionally | Often | Consistently

Context: Being able to forgive someone for a wrongdoing, whether it was intentional or unintentional, has been shown to be an important character trait in building trust relationships in our personal and professional life – especially in leaders.[148]

Key point: We all make mistakes, and at times we will need others to forgive us. Practising forgiveness shows our empathy for others, which helps us add depth and meaning to our relationships.

Activity: This week, think of a mistake or wrongdoing that you've experienced. Ask yourself this question: What would cause a reasonable person to make this mistake? Try to place yourself in their shoes (with their competence and in their situation) … really work on having empathy with them. If possible (and it won't always be easy or in extreme situations, even possible for you), see if you can forgive them for the wrongdoing.

Evidence: Researchers have shown that forgiveness is strongly associated with our sense of wellbeing, including feeling less depressed, boosting positivity, improving relationships, enhancing our sense of meaning in life, and sense of personal empowerment.[149]

22. Kindness

This includes your sense of wanting to regularly find ways to make life better for others.

Never | Rarely | Occasionally | Often | Consistently

Context: The importance of being kind to others is something most of us have been taught since an early age. Kindness is steeped in religion ("clothe yourselves with compassion, kindness, humility, gentleness and patience", Colossians 3:12); kindness is widely discussed in philosophy (Aristotle defined kindness as "helpfulness towards someone in need, not in return for anything, nor for the advantage of the helper himself, but for that of the person helped");[150] and researchers in positive psychology have found kindness to be strongly associated with our wellbeing.[151]

Key point: It is hard to argue with the fact that when someone shows us kindness, we feel good and it enhances our view of what is positive in the world. Each of us can take the personal responsibility to enhance others' view of what is positive in the world by practising more acts of kindness.

Activity: Rather than patronise you here by suggesting some random acts of kindness that you could do, you already know how to be kind … be kind.

Evidence: Whatever act of kindness you decide to do, whether planned or random, be mindful in the moment – watch the response of the other person and notice the physical and emotional responses you personally experience. There's no denying it – being kind is good for the other person, but undoubtedly good for the person practising the act of kindness.

23. Humour

This includes your sense of fun in the world and, while not ignoring difficult experiences, wanting to mostly look on the light side of life.

Never | Rarely | Occasionally | Often | Consistently

Context: Louis Armstrong beautifully sang the words "When you're smiling, the whole world smiles with you". Humour enriches our lives in two ways: when we experience it ourselves and when we give it to others. Take care in using sarcasm; while it can be positive in trust-based relationships, it can create conflict where trust is low.[152]

Key point: Some people tell themselves that they aren't naturally funny people; however, most of us can see humour in the world ... if we care to look for it and allow ourselves to experience it.

Activity: Going through your normal day, purposefully and consciously try and find something that makes you smile.

Evidence: When you experience humour, notice what's happening to you physically and emotionally, but also take note of what's happening to the people around you – humour is infectious.

24. Values

This includes your sense of clarity of who you are and what you stand for in this world and the guiding principles by which you choose your decisions and actions.

Never | Rarely | Occasionally | Often | Consistently

Context: When we are clear on our personal values they provide us with direction and a blueprint toward appropriate action that can help us strive to be at our best and achieve meaningful life goals – especially when we are experiencing difficult thoughts and feelings.

Key point: Life isn't always easy, and without clarity of your personal values to guide you in difficult times on appropriate actions to strive to be at your best, the danger is you get hooked into your difficult thoughts and feelings, which can cause you to move away from striving to be the best version of yourself.

Activity: Revisit the work you did in chapter seven and reflect on the day you've had so far. Ask yourself, 'What actions have I taken today that demonstrate each of my core personal values?' (Note: If you still haven't arrived at your core personal values, I recommend you complete that as the activity.)

Evidence: Clarity of personal values is in itself a rewarding experience and enhances your sense of self-determination. This releases your intrinsic motivation to achieve in life and nurtures your relationships through the demonstration of 'good' character and consistency in values-aligned behaviour. Together, these form two of the three essential elements required for trustworthiness (the third being a demonstration of your competence).

25. Emotional intelligence

This extends your emotional agility to include your sense of empathy and understanding of not only your own emotions, but the emotions of others, and choosing appropriate behaviour that supports and adds value to your relationships.

Never | Rarely | Occasionally | Often | Consistently

Context: Your emotional intelligence is demonstrated through a combination of four abilities: (1) how well you can perceive or identify emotions in yourself and in others, (2) how well you can base your thinking, decisions, and actions while considering your emotions and the emotions of others, (3) how well you can understand your emotions and those of others, and (4) how well you can manage your emotions and those of others.[153]

Key point: Living a 'good life' means experiencing a range of emotions, and certainly not only those that make us feel good. Emotions such as anger, sadness, frustration, and fear are not 'negative' emotions; given certain situations, these types of emotions are appropriate (we always need to be mindful of the consequences of our actions on ourselves and on others – this is an important part of emotional intelligence – our choice of actions based on our emotions).

Activity: Throughout your day today, consciously 'name' any emotion that you feel (make a note of them) … see how many different emotions you become consciously aware of in the day.

Use the following emotional labels (based on research by Cowen and colleagues)[154] as a guide: adoration, amusement, anger, awe, confusion, contempt, contentment, desire, disappointment, disgust, distress, ecstasy, elation, embarrassment, fear, interest, pain, realisation, relief, sadness, surprise (negative), surprise (positive), sympathy, triumph, guilt, pride, romantic love, serenity, shame.

Evidence: As you complete this activity you will become more aware of your emotions, what triggers them, and how you act when experiencing each emotion.

Where to from here?

My online and home-office libraries are bursting with books and folders with research articles on the evidence-based research around living more happy, meaningful, flourishing, and prosperous lives.

Just to remind you, my intention here isn't to replicate all that research, but to provide you with these 25 contributing elements that you can repeatedly come back to and take some action on.

In researching and sharing with you these elements that contribute to a meaningful, flourishing, and prosperous life – to living a 'good' life – it's often been like holding a mirror up to myself and challenging myself to take action on areas I need to personally work on.

My wish and hope for you is that you come back and revisit this chapter time and time again and select from it one contributing element to living in the light of day to work on.

Chapter Ten Summary

There are many elements that contribute to your overall sense of life satisfaction and well-being. Mindfully choosing which contributing elements will help you strive to be at your personal best and taking appropriate values-aligned action on those contributing elements provides daily mindful actions that will boost your sense of well-being and life satisfaction.

"There are only two ways to live your life. One is as though nothing is a miracle. The other is as though everything is a miracle."

Albert Einstein

Chapter Eleven

It's not like a take-away pizza

When I studied for a Master's degree in Professional Ethics, my lecturer, Professor Stephen Cohen, opened the first lecture by saying:

"Ethics is not like a take-away pizza … discuss."

He then left the room for an hour.

On his return, after my cohort and I had determined a host of interpretations and meanings behind his statement, he said this:

"We are all meaning-makers. We can find meaning in almost anything, if not in everything."

To this day, I find those words so powerful. We can look at almost anything in our lives, and if we put our minds and imagination to it, we can find something meaningful about it.

As I'm writing now, I have just returned from my daily walk through the bayside park near our home. On my walk a magpie flew by and landed just near the path and commenced carolling (the sound a magpie makes is not a chirp, it sounds like they swallowed a chorus of birds, and they all sing at once). I stopped, watched and listened, and as I now reflect on that, the meaning I find in the experience is how often in this fast-paced world we miss some of the amazing things that are going on around us … and I can use this memory as a reminder to stop, watch, listen, and be present.

Ok … I realise that might sound like a bit of a ramble, but I'm hoping you get my point.

Why not try it out as an activity now … have a look around you. What do you see or hear? Something will quickly grab your attention, maybe more than everything else. Focus on it for a moment and ask yourself, 'What's the meaning I can make out of this?' Or, said another way, 'What's the lesson I can learn?'

Yes, we are meaning makers and when we seek meaning from our lives, whether through relationships, work, hobbies, learning, or everyday experiences, we make life more meaningful … more full of meaning – and as you have discovered in this book, a meaningful life is a part of a living a 'good' life.

Toby Green wrote a song titled 'Don't let the old man in', and there's a line that I reckon is a cracker … he sings:

"Many moons I have lived

My body's weathered and worn

Ask yourself how old you'd be

If you didn't know the day you were born"

If you didn't know when you were born, take a moment to think about how old you feel.

I certainly don't feel like I am in my sixties, and yet I am … and I'm comfortable with that. I've been blessed with good emotional and physical health. Along the way I've had some terrible experiences that knocked the wind out of my sails, and some exhilaratingly positive experiences that have filled my sails with wind.

Ok … enough of the yachting analogy (I don't even sail).

But what I'm saying is, sometimes it's easy to just exist, to let life pass us by and forget what a blessing it is to be alive.

That's the meaning of the magpie story right there!

In John Lennon's song 'Beautiful Boy' he wrote and sang the words, "Life is what happens to you while you're busy making other plans", and I reckon he got it right.

So many of us, me included at times, forget to be present. It's so easy to get caught up in everything and miss so much.

Let me share with you another example of meaning making.

In the year Neil Armstrong set foot on the moon, I was in my fourth year at a Catholic primary school and was taught by nuns. Once a week, though, the parish priest, Father Muldoon (don't worry … this is a happy story), would drop in and ask my class a question.

On this day, the question was, "Which part of a shoe is the most important part, and why?"

The answers my classmates came up with included:

- **the laces – because they hold everything together**
- **the leather – because that's what it's made from**
- **the toe – because it comes first**
- **the sole – because everything stands on it**
- **the person – because they are wearing it.**

Now I reckon all of these are pretty good answers, and I remember at the time I didn't contribute anything.

However, as each class member gave their answer, Father Muldoon would say, "Yes … that's a great answer, but it is not the answer I am looking for".

Finally, Father Muldoon shared with us his answer: "The most important part of a shoe is the back of the heel".

The reason we were given was that the back of the heel is the last thing people see when you leave the room, and yet it's the part of the shoe that many people fail to look after.

Now, regardless of whether you agree with that answer or not, let me remind you of what Professor Stephen Cohen shared with our class: "We are all meaning-makers".

Even aged around nine years of age, my classmates came up with a number of answers to the same question. All good answers, and all with good meaning or reasons for their answers.

At the time of writing this book, Father Muldoon asked our class that question over 50 years ago, and it still sticks in my mind. (I know … you have no idea the stuff that pops into my head.)

Here's the thing, though … I've attached a different meaning to that story – what I now refer to as *'the philosophy of the shoe'*.

When we leave this 'room of life', the back of the heel is a metaphor for the way we have lived our life … it's the legacy we leave in the memories of those we have impacted during our life – our family, friends, work colleagues, customers, and whoever else we might have connected with.

I wrote this book as a reminder for you, me, and everyone else that we have a chance to live a 'good' life, to continually strive to be the best version of ourselves.

While again, none of us is perfect, we will make mistakes, some days will be great, and others will be horrible.

And that's life, isn't it.

None of us knows what the future holds – it's an illusion.

All we really have is what we've experienced, what we have, the relationships we are blessed to be in, and what we choose to do and who we choose to be ... in the present, now, today.

Not for one minute do I believe this book has all the answers to living a 'good' life, but what I do hope is that you have found some value, that you will take some action and be inspired to continually strive to be the best version you can be of yourself ... the world needs that.

As an author, though, what's most important to me is you.

So, let me leave you with this personal invitation. Let me know how you're going with living in the light of day. Visit my website and share your feedback, questions or comments: www.davidpenglase.com

For now, my best to you.

Acknowledgements

It is said it takes a village to raise a child, and as an author I have learned it takes a cohort of wise and experienced colleagues and friends to help produce a book worthy of readership. With some 'humble arrogance', I have no hesitation in saying this book is the best I have written and in many ways is the culmination of my life's work and learning so far.

It has also been a project where I have received caring guidance and advice and have been so wonderfully supported.

I want to acknowledge and thank Blaise van Hecke, the founder of Busybird Publishing, who when I first presented my manuscript for Living in the Light of Day to Blaise, her encouragement was inspiring. We were only in the early stages of the publishing process, when I learned from Blaise's husband (and Busybird's Studio Manager) Kev Howlett, that Blaise had sadly and unexpectedly passed away.

To Kev, who is courageously continuing Blaise's work and legacy with Busybird Publishing, you've been my patient and caring guide through the publishing of Living in the Light of Day. I thank you and am inspired by your resilience, grit, and professionalism.

The editing process for any book is important, and I want to thank Heather Kelly for her skill, and keen eye to detail for editing the book.

Thank you to Nikki Davis from Index Your Book, for your guidance, timeliness, and professional work on indexing Living in the Light of Day.

To Dale Druckman who I have only known for a short time and I look forward to many more coffee catchups. Thank you for sharing your wisdom and many years of experience with the book publishing and distribution industry.

A big thank you to Professor Mike Steger, Dr Tim Lomas, Dr Simon Longstaff AO, Peter Baines OAM, Olivia Sarah-Le Lacheur, Dr Adam Fraser, Major Matina Jewell (retd), Larry Fingleson, Shawn Hunter, Jon Yeo, and Nicolette Barnard for taking time out of your busy schedules and lives to read the advanced copies of Living in the Light of Day and for providing your testimonials, allowing readers a glimpse into what to expect and gain from the book.

Finally, the unwavering support, patience, and love that I have and continue to receive from Liz, my best friend, wife and business partner, you know how much you mean to me, I thank you, and am so blessed to have you by my side.

References and Notations

1 Altridge, M. (2019). A global perspective in promoting workplace mental health and the role of employee assistance programs. American Journal of Health Promotion, 34(4), 622-627

2 Thorsteinsen, K., & Vitterso, J. (2018). Striving for wellbeing: The different roles of hedonia and eudaimonia in goal pursuit and goal achievement. *International Journal of Wellbeing*, 8(2), 89-109.

3 Mete, E. S. (2019). The Relationship among Altruism, Affective Commitment, Job Satisfaction, and Turnover Intention: A Research on Boundary Spanning Positions in Hotel Enterprises, *Journal of Tourism and Gastronomy Studies*, 7(1), 310-327.

4 Angel P, Jenkins A, Stephens A. Understanding entrepreneurial success: A phenomenographic approach. *International Small Business Journal*. 2018;36(6):611-636.

5 Hall, V. (2007). *The truth about trust in business.* Entente Pty Ltd. Sydney.

6 Clark, L. (2013). 'Lance Armstrong admits doping in Oprah Winfrey interview, AP reports'. *The Washington Post*, 14 January. https://www.washingtonpost.com/sports/lance-armstrong-admits-doping-in-oprah-winfrey-interview-ap-reports/2013/01/14/a635a424-5eaf-11e2-9940-6fc488f3fecd_story.html

7 CNN Wire Staff (2012). 'Schwarzenegger admits habit of keeping secrets, including multiple affairs', 2 October. https://edition.cnn.com/2012/09/30/us/schwarzenegger-interview/index.html

8 Ziffer, D. (2019). 'NAB bosses come in for special criticism from banking royal commissioner Kenneth Hayne', 5 February. https://www.abc.net.au/news/2019-02-05/nab-bosses-singled-out-banking-royal-commission-final-report/10779324

9 https://abcnews.go.com/Business/theranos-ceo-elizabeth-holmes-600-times-broadcast-deposition/story?id=60576630

10 Berger, A. (2009). Brandeis and the History of Transparency. https://sunlightfoundation.com/2009/05/26/brandeis-and-the-history-of-transparency

11 Pagano, A. (1987). Criteria for Ethical Decision Making in Managerial Situations. SSRN Electronic Journal. 10.2139/ssrn.1708237.

12 Sims, R. (Chair ACCC) (2018). Giblin Lecture. 'Companies behaving badly?', 13 July. https://www.accc.gov.au/speech/companies-behaving-badly

13 Rushton, K. (2013). 'Wolf of Wall Street: Reformed but far from sheepish'. *The Sydney Morning Herald*, 9 December. https://www.smh.com.au/money/investing/wolf-of-wall-street-reformed-but-far-from-sheepish-20131209-2z0wx.html

14 Indra Nooyi. Former Chair and CEO of PepsiCo. https://www.linkedin.com/in/indranooyi/

15 Uchino, B. N., Cacioppo, J. T., & Kiecolt-Glaser, J. K. (1996). 'The relationship between social support and psychological processes: A review with emphasis on underlying mechanisms and implications for health'. *Psychological Bulletin,* 119(3), 488-531.

16 Diener, E., & Seligman, M. E. P. (2002). 'Very happy people'. *Psychological Science,* 13(1), 81-84.

17 Ryan, R. M., & Deci, E. L. (2017). *Self-determination theory: Basic psychological needs in motivation, development, and wellness.* Guilford Publishing, New York, NY.

18 Frankl, V. E. (2006). *Man's search for meaning*. Beacon Press, Boston, MA.

19 Edelman Trust Barometer 2018.

20 Botsman, R. (2017). *Who can you trust? How technology brought us together – and why it could drive us apart.* Hatchett Book Group, New York, NY.

21 *The Sydney Morning Herald*: Volkswagen – 23 September 2015; Facebook – 4 October 2018; Banking – 15 August 2018.

22 Royal Commission into Misconduct in the Banking, Superannuation and Financial Services Industry (2019). Commonwealth of Australia.

23 Covey, S. R. (1990). *The 7 habits of highly effective people.* The Business Library (Imprint of Information Australia), Melbourne, Australia.

24 Isenman, L. (2013). 'Understanding unconscious intelligence and intuition'. *Perspectives in Biology and Medicine,* 56(1), 148-166.

25 Kaiser, T., Del Guidice, M., & Booth, T. (2019). 'Global sex differences in personality: Replication with an open online dataset'. *Journal of Personality,* 88(3), 415-429.

26 Mattarozzi, K., Todrov, A., Marzocchi, M., Vicari, A., & Russo, P. (2015). 'Effects of gender and personality of first impressions'. *Plos one.10.* eo135529.10.1371/journal.pone.0135529.

27 Ambady, N., & Rosenthal, R. (1992). 'Thin slices of expressive behaviour as predictors of interpersonal consequences: A meta-analysis'. *Psychological Bulletin,* 111(2), 256-274.

28 Baker, A., Porter, S., Ten Brinke, L., & Mundy, C. (2016). 'Seeing is believing: Observer perceptions of trait trustworthiness predict perceptions of honesty in high stakes emotional appeals'. *Psychology, Crime & Law. DOI:*10.1080/1068316X.2016.1190844

29 http://www.jimrohn.com

30 Uauy, R., & Lock, K. (2006). 'Commentary: The importance of addressing the rise of overweight and obesity—progress or lack of action during the last fifty years? *International Journal of Epidemiology, 35(1),* 18–20. https://doi.org/10.1093/ije/dyi266

31 The cane toad (Bufo marinus) – fact sheet. Department of the Environment, Water, Heritage and the Arts, 2010. https://www.environment.gov.au/biodiversity/invasive-species/publications/factsheet-cane-toad-bufo-marinus

32 Longstaff, S., & Whitaker, V. (2018). *Trust, legitimacy & the ethical foundations of the market economy.* The Ethics Centre.

33 Batson, C. D. (2011). *Altruism in humans.* Oxford University Press, New York, NY.

34 Post, S. (2005). 'Altruism, happiness, and health: It's good to be good'. *International Journal of Behavioral Medicine,* 12(2), 66–77.

35 Seligman, M. E. P. (2002). *Authentic happiness: Using the new positive psychology to realize your potential for lasting fulfillment.* Free Press, New York, NY.

36 Ricard, M. (2017). 'Altruism and happiness'. In *Happiness: Transforming the development landscape.* . The Centre for Bhutan Studies and GNH, pp. 156-158.

37 Penglase, D. (2016). 'The impact of intentional prosocial behaviour on meaning, motivation and life satisfaction in a workplace setting'. Dissertation thesis. MScAPP. University of East London.

38 Ryan, R. M., & Deci, E. L. (2017). *Self-determination theory: Basic psychological needs in motivation, development and wellness.* The Guilford Press, New York, NY.

39 https://www.ted.com/talks/simon_sinek_how_great_leaders_inspire_action?language=en

40 Sinek, S. (2009). *Start with WHY: How great leaders inspire everyone to take action.* Penguin, New York, NY.

41 Anscomb, G. E. M. (1957). *Intention.* Harvard University Press, London, England.

42 Gollwitzer, P. M., & Sheeran, P. (2006). 'Implementation intentions and goal achievement: A meta-analysis of effects and processes'. *Advances in Experimental Social Psychology,* 38, 69-119.

43 Gollwitzer, P. M., & Brandstatter, V. (1997). 'Implementation intentions and effective goal pursuit'. *Journal of Personality and Social Psychology,* 73(1), 186-199.

44 Cancer Australia report (2015). *Early detection of breast cancer.* https://canceraustralia.gov.au/publications-and-resources/position-statements/early-detection-breast-cancer

45 Prestwich, A. J., Conner, M. T., Lawton, R. J., Bailey, W., Litman, J., & Molyneaux, V. (2005). 'Individual and collaborative implementation intentions and the promotion of breast self-examination'. *Psychology and Health, 20*(6), 743-760.

46 Milne, S. E., Orbell, S., & Sheeran, P. (2002). 'Combining motivational and volitional interventions to promote exercise participation: Protection motivation theory and implementation intentions'. *British Journal of Health Psychology,* 7, 163-184.

47 Frankl, V. (1946). *Man's search for meaning.* Beacon Press, Boston, MA.

48 Steger, M. F. (2009). 'Meaning in life'. In CR Snyder, & SJ Lopez (Eds.), *The Oxford handbook of positive psychology,* 2nd edition. Oxford University Press, New York, NY, pp. 679-687.

49 Baumeister, R. F. (2005). *The cultural animal: Human nature, meaning, and social life.* Oxford University Press, New York, NY.

50 Baumeister, R. F., & Vohs, K. D. (2002). 'The pursuit of meaningfulness in life'. In C R Snyder & SJ Lopez (Eds.), *The Oxford handbook of positive psychology,* 2nd edition. Oxford University Press, New York,NY, pp. 608–618.

51 Hunter, G. S. (2016). *Small acts of leadership: 12 intentional behaviors that lead to big impact.* Bibliomotion, Brookline, MA.

52 Edelman Trust Barometer (2018).

53 Ernst & Young global trust in the workplace survey. https://www.de.ey.com/gl/en/about-us/our-people-and-culture/ey-global-study-trust-in-the-workplace

54 Hooton, A. (2018). 'Other people's money'. *The Sydney Morning Herald Good Weekend,* 21 July.

55 Kethledge, R. M., & Erwin, M. S. (2018). *Lead yourself first: Inspiring leadership through solitude.* Bloomsbury Publishing, New York, NY.

56 https://hbr.org/2019/08/6-reasons-we-make-bad-decisions-and-what-to-do-about-them

57 Botsman, R. (2017). *Who can you trust: How technology brought us together and why it might drive us apart.* Hachette Book Group, New York, NY.

58 'News use across social media platforms 2018'. Pew Research Center. https://www.journalism.org/2018/09/10/news-use-across-social-media-platforms-2018/

59 Couturier, K and Tabuchi, H. (2016). The Airbag in Your Car Could Explode. This is what you should do about it. *The New York Times.* www.nytimes.com/interactive/2016/business/takata-airbag-recall-guide.html

60 http://www.foodauthority.nsw.gov.au/fp/food-poisoning

61 http://www.cdc.gov/foodborneburden/index.html

62 Holland, D., and Mahmoudzadeh, N. (2020) Foodborne Disease Estimates for the United Kingdom 2018. *U.K. Food Standard Agency.*

63 https://mccrindle.com.au/insights/blog/fast-facts-marriages-australia/

64 https://legaljobs.io/blog/divorce-rate-in-america/

65 McKinsey & Company (2020). A Global view of how consumer behaviour is changing amid Covid-19

66 www.statista.com/topics/871/online-shopping

67 www.statista.com/statistics/867037/australia-loss-of-online-shopping-scams

68 https://www.pwc.fr/fr/assets/files/pdf/2015/05/pwc_etude_sharing_economy.pdf

69 https://press.airbnb.com/about-us/

70 https://housemethod.com/lifestyle/airbnb-guests-breaking-the-rules/

71 McBride, S. (2019). 'Uber's nightmare has just begun'. *Forbes.com*, 4 September.

72 Siddiqui, F. (2019). Internal data shows Uber's reputation hasn't changed much since #DeleteUber. *WashingtonPost.com*, 29 August.

73 https://www.pwc.com.au/people/megatrends/trust.html

74 *Lewicki, R. J., & Bunker, B. B. (1995).* 'Trust in relationships: A model of trust development and decline.' In BB Bunker, & JZ Rubin (Eds.), *Conflict, cooperation and justice.* Jossey-Bass, San Francisco,CA, pp.133-173.

75 https://en.oxforddictionaries.com/definition/trust

76 Steger, M. F. (2009). 'Meaning in life'. In SJ Lopez, &CR Snyder (Eds.), *The Oxford handbook of positive psychology*, 2nd edition. Oxford University Press, New York, NY.

77 Steger, M. F., Kashdan, T. B., Sullivan, B. A., & Lorentz, D. (2008). 'Understanding the search for meaning in life: Personality, cognitive style, and the dynamic between seeking and experiencing meaning'. *Journal of Personality*, 76(2), April.

78 Steger, M. F., Frazier, P., Oishi, S., & Kaler, M. (2006). 'The meaning in life questionnaire: Assessing the presence of and search for meaning in life'. *Journal of Counseling Psychology, 53*, 80-93.

79 Seligman, M. E. P. (2011). *Flourish: A new understanding of happiness and wellbeing – and how to achieve them.* Nicholas Brealey Publishing, London, UK.

80 Peck, M. S. (1978). *The road less travelled: A new psychology of love, traditional values, and spiritual growth.* Simon & Schuster, New York, NY.

81 Brown, B. (2010). *The gifts of imperfection: Let go of who you think you're supposed to be and embrace who you are.* Hazelden, Center City, MI.

82 Moores, T. T., & Chang, J. C. (2009). 'Self-efficacy, overconfidence, and the negative effect on subsequent performance: A field study'. *Information and Management, 46(2),* 69-76.

83 https://www.eharmony.com/online-dating-statistics

84 http:www.stress.org/42-worrying-workplace-stress-statistics-2

85 http://www.mentalhealth.org.uk/our-work/mental-health-workplace

86 State of Workplace Mental Health Australia (2019). https://www.headsup.org.au/docs/default-source/resources/bl1270-report---tns-the-state-of-mental-health-in-australian-workplaces-hr.pdf?sfvrsn=8

87 Wehmeyer, M. L. (2004). 'Beyond self-determination: Causal agency theory'. *Journal of Developmental and Physical Disabilities, 16*(4), 337-359.

88 Lyubomirsky, S. (2007). *The how of happiness: A new approach to getting the life you want.* Penguin Books, New York, NY.

89 Sheldon, K. M., & Lyubomirsky, S. (2007). 'Is it possible to become happier? And if so, how?'. *Social and Personality Psychology Compass, 1/1, 129–145.*

90 https://www.psychologytoday.com/ca/blog/curious/201508/what-really-makes-you-happy-person

91 Brown, N. J. L., Rohrer, J. M. (2019). 'Easy as (happiness) pie? A critical evaluation of a popular model of the determinants of wellbeing'. *Journal of Happiness Studies,* 9 May.

92 Newman, K. M. (2020). 'How much of your happiness is under your control?' *Greater Good Magazine,* 18 February. https://greatergood.berkeley.edu/article/item/how_much_of_your_happiness_is_under_your_control

93 DeSteno, D. (2014). *The truth about trust: How it determines success in life, love, learning, and more.* Hudson Street Press, New York, NY.

94 Gecas, V. (1989). 'The social psychology of self-efficacy'. *Annual Reviews of Sociology,* 15, 291-316.

95 Maddux, J. E. (2009). 'The power of believing you can'. In S J Lopez, & C R Snyder (Eds.), *The Oxford handbook of positive psychology,* 2nd edition. Oxford University Press, New York, NY (pp. 335-343).

96 https://selfdeterminationtheory.org/theory/

97 Harris, R. (2011). *The reality slap: How to find fulfilment when life hurts.* Exisle Publishing Limited, Wollombi, Australia.

98 Carlzon, J. (1989). *Moments of truth: New strategies for today's consumer-economy.* Harper Collins, New York, NY.

99 Harris, R. (2019). Act made simple: *An easy-to-read primer on acceptance and commitment therapy.* New Harbinger Publications, Oakland, CA.

100 Wood, J. V., Perunovic, W. Q. E., & Lee, J. W. (2009). 'Positive self-statements: Power for some, peril for others. *Psychological Science, 20*(7), 860-866.

101 Hayes, S. C. (2019). *A liberated mind: How to pivot toward what matters.* Avery, New York, NY.

102 Maltz, M. (1960). *Psycho-cybernetics.* Prentice-Hall, Englewood Cliffs, NJ.

103 *VV Gouveia, V. V., Vione, K. C., Milfont, T. L., & Fishcer, R. (2015).* 'Patterns of value change during the life span: Some evidence from a functional approach to values'. *Personality and Social Psychology Bulletin,* 41(9), 1276-1290.

104 Kaftan, O. J., & Freund, A. M. (2018). 'The way is the goal: The role of goal focus for successful goal pursuit and subjective wellbeing'. In E Diener, S Oishi, L Tay (Eds.), *Handbook of wellbeing.* DEF Publishers, Salt Lake City, UT, online.

105 Fraser, A. (2020). *Strive: Embracing the gift of the struggle.* Wiley, Qld.

106 Gill, H., Boies, K., Finegan, J. E., & McNally, J. (2005). 'Antecedents of trust: Establishing a boundary condition for the relation between propensity to trust and intention to trust'. *Journal of Business and Psychology, 19*(3), 287-302.

107 Fetchenhauer, D., & Dunning, D. (2009). 'Do people trust too much or too little?' *Journal of Economic Psychology,* 30, 263–276.

108 Global trust in professions, (2019). August. https://www.ipsos.com/en-au/its-fact-scientists-are-most-trusted-people-world

109 Dunn, J., Ruedy, N. E., & Schweitzer, M. E. (2012). 'It hurts both ways: How social comparisons harm affective and cognitive trust'. *Organizational Behavior and Human Decision Processes,* 117, 2-14.

110 Mayzlin, D., Dover, Y., & Chevalier, J. (2014). 'Promotional reviews: An empirical investigation of online review manipulation. *American Economic Review,* 104(8), 2421–2455.

111 https://www.fakespot.com/

112 https://reviewmeta.com/

113 Berg, J., Dickhaut, J., & McCabe, K. (1995). 'Trust, reciprocity, and social history'. *Games and Economic Behavior.* 10, 122-142.

114 Greenberg, M. (2012). 'The six attributes of courage'. *Psychology Today, 23 August.* https://www.psychologytoday.com/au/blog/the-mindful-self-express/201208/the-six-attributes-courage

115 Deloitte Access Economics (2014). *The collaborative economy.* https://www2.deloitte.com/content/dam/Deloitte/au/Documents/Economics/deloitte-au-economics-collaborative-economy-google-170614.pdf

116 Cisco Whitepaper (2017). *Workplace collaboration in Australia and New Zealand: Trends, behaviours and impact.* https://www.cisco.com/c/dam/global/en_au/assets/pdfs/workplace-collaboration-in-AU-and-NZ-2018.pdf

117 https://www.washingtonpost.com/opinions/2020/03/25/lets-make-sure-this-crisis-doesnt-go-waste/

118 https://www.theguardian.com/technology/2020/mar/13/covid-19-could-cause-permanent-shift-toward-home-working

119 https://globalworkplaceanalytics.com/whitepapers

120 https://www.viacharacter.org/faq Understanding key terms - What is character?

121 Peterson, C., & Seligman, M. E. P. (2004). *Character strengths and virtues: A classification and handbook.* Oxford University Press, New York, NY/ American Psychological Association, Washington, DC.

122 https://www.mayersonfoundation.org/

123 https://www.viacharacter.org/

124 Hinman, L. M. (1998). *Ethics: A pluralistic approach to moral theory.* Harcourt Brace College Publishers, Orlando, FL.

125 Compton, W. C., & Hoffman, E. (2013). *Positive psychology: The science of happiness and flourishing*, Cengage Learning, Belmont, CA.

126 Seligman, M. E. P. (2011). *Flourish: A new understanding of happiness and wellbeing – and how to achieve them.* Nicholas Brealey Publishing, London, UK.

127 Lomas, T., Hefferon, K., & Ivtzan, I. (2014). *Applied positive psychology: Integrated positive practice*, Sage Publications, London.

128 David, S. A., Boniwell, I., & Conley Ayers, A. (2013). *The Oxford handbook of happiness.* Oxford University Press, Oxford, UK.

129 Cantril, H. (1965). *The pattern of human concerns.* Rutgers University Press, New Brunswick, NJ.

130 *Diener, E., Emmons, R., Larsen, R., & Griffen, S. (1985).* 'The satisfaction with life scale'. *Journal of Personality Assessment,* 49, 71-75.

131 Biswas-Diener, R. (2010). *Practicing positive psychology coaching: Assessment, activities, and strategies for success.* John Wiley & Sons Inc, Hoboken, NJ.

132 Ryff, C. D., & Keyes, C. L. M. (1995). 'The structure of psychological wellbeing revisited'. *Journal of Personality and Social Psychology*, 69, 719-727.

133 Seligman, M. E. P. (2011). *Flourish: A new understanding of happiness and wellbeing – and how to achieve them.* Nicholas Brealey Publishing, London, UK.

134 Ryan, R. M., & Deci, E. L. (2017). *Self-determination theory: Basic psychological needs in motivation, development, and wellness.* The Guilford Press, New York, NY.

135 Rath, T., & Harter, J. (2010). *Wellbeing: The five essential elements.* Gallup Press, New York, NY.

136 Lawrence, P. R., & Nitin, N. (2002). *Driven: How human nature shapes our choices.* Jossey-Bass, San Francisco, CA.

137 Huppert, F. A., & So, T. T. C. (2009). 'What percentage of people in Europe are flourishing and what characterises them?' Prepared for the OECD/ISQOLS meeting, 'Measuring subjective wellbeing: an opportunity for NSWs?', Florence – 23/24 July. Well-being Institute, University of Cambridge, Cambridge, UK.

138 Mariappan, R., & Subramanian, M. R. (2019). 'Experimental investigation of cognitive impact of yoga meditation on physical and mental health parameters using electro encephalogram'. In *Soft computing and medical bioinformatics. Springer Briefs in Applied Sciences and Technology.* Springer, Singapore.

139 Dunn, E., & Norton, M. (2013). Happy money: The new science of smarter spending. One World Publications, London, UK

140 Hely, S. (2018). 'Why 86% of Australians don't know their monthly expenses'. *Money Magazine,* 21 February. https://www.moneymag.com.au/86-australians-dont-know-expenses

141 Dunn, E., & Norton, M. (2013). *Happy money: The new science of smarter spending.* One World Publications, London, UK.

142 Seligman, M. E. P. (1990). *Learned optimism: How to change your mind and your life.* Vintage Books, New York, NY.

143 Kosfeld, M., Heinrichs, M., Zak, P. J., Fischbacher, U., & Fehr E. (2005). 'Oxytocin increases trust in humans'. *Zurich open repository and archive.* University of Zurich, Zurich, Switzerland.

144 Rath, T., & Harter, J. (2010). *Wellbeing: The five essential elements.* Gallup Press, New York, NY.

145 Kashdan, T. (2009). *Curious. Discover the missing ingredient to a fulfilling life.* Harper Publishing, New York, NY.

146 McGonigal, K. (2012). *The will power instinct: How self-control works, why it matters, and what you can do to get more of it.* Penguin Group, London, UK.

147 Cloud, H. (2006). *Integrity: The courage to meet the demands of reality.* Harper Collins, New York, NY.

148 Caldwell, C., & Dixon, R. D. (2010). 'Love, forgiveness, and trust: Critical values of the modern leader'. *Journal of Business Ethics*, 93, 91–101.

149 Akhtar, S., Dolan, A., & Barlow, J. (2017). 'Understanding the relationship between state forgiveness and psychological wellbeing: A qualitative study'. *Journal of Religion and Health,* 56(2), 450–463. DOI 10.1007/s10943-016-0188-9.

150 Ross, W. D. (2010). *Rhetoric.* (W Rhys Roberts, Translator; WD Ross, Editor.) Cosimo Classics, New York, NY.

151 Lyubomirsky, S. (2007). *The how of happiness: A new approach to getting the life you want.* Penguin Books, New York, NY.

152 Huang, L., Gino, F., & Galinsky, A. D. (2015). 'The highest form of intelligence: Sarcasm increases creativity for both expressers and recipients'. *Organizational Behavior and Human Decision Processes,* 131, 162-177.

153 Salovey, P., Mayer, J. D., Caruso, D., & Yoo, S. H. (2009). 'The positive psychology of emotional intelligence'. In SJ Lopez, & CR Snyder (Eds.), *The Oxford handbook of positive psychology,* 2nd edition. Oxford University Press, New York, NY, pp. 237-248.

154 Cowen, A. S., Elfenbein, H. A., Laukka, P., & Keltner, D (2019). 'Mapping 24 emotions conveyed by brief human vocalization'. *American Psychologist,* 74(6), 698–712.

INDEX